THE INTERNET

in easy steps

Geoff Preston

COMPUTER
STEP

In easy steps is an imprint of Computer Step
Southfield Road. Southam
Warwickshire CV47 OFB. England

Tel: 01926 817999 Fax: 01926 817005
http://www.computerstep.com

Notice of Liability

Every effort has been made to ensure that this book contains accurate
and current information. However, Computer Step and the author shall
not be liable for any loss or damage suffered by readers as a result of
any information contained herein.

Trademarks

All trademarks are acknowledged as belonging to their respective
companies.

Printed and bound in the United Kingdom

ISBN 1-84078-066-5

Contents

Email 75

5

Newsgroups

6

Interaction

7

Bargains for all?

8

See me, hear me

Music on the Web

Downloading

Do-it-yourself

Finance on the Web

13

Internet shopping

14

Food and drink

15

16 Healthy living — 241

17 Children's websites — 259

18 Education — 283

Introduction

This chapter introduces the Internet and describes the level of detail that this book goes into.

Covers

Chapter One

Who should read this book?

If you're standing in a bookshop reading this introduction and trying to find out if this is really the book you want, here are a couple of pointers which should make the task a little easier.

Do you want to know about SMTP, POP3 and TCP/IP protocols? If the answer is 'yes', then close the book, put it back on the shelf and look elsewhere. *The Internet in easy steps* will be of no use to you whatsoever.

This book is not for techno-freaks.

If, on the other hand, you want to know how to use the Internet effectively and how to make the most of its services, and indeed find out what services are available, then look no further. This is probably the book you need.

What is the Internet?

The name 'Internet' is a very appropriate title. An INTERnational NETwork of computers containing a huge fount of knowledge which anyone with a computer and a telephone line can access.

Internet statistics are mind-boggling. One estimate suggests that the amount of material on the Net doubles every couple of months. Another claim is that every few seconds another individual from somewhere in the world becomes an Internet subscriber. Of the hundreds of websites that are added daily, some are quickly forgotten about, but many thrive.

This indeed is the information super-highway but just as anyone can search the Internet for the information they require, so too can anyone contribute to the global resource of knowledge. Free speech now takes on a whole new meaning. Anyone can put anything on the Internet which can then be accessed worldwide. Pornography, anarchistic philosophies, riot incitement, explosives manufacture – you name it, it's sure to be there. Even sites which do not contain material of this type vary in quality enormously.

But that is the appeal of the Internet.

A server is a main computer used to hold data and program files used by other computers attached to it on a network.

Servers owned and managed by organisations (Internet Service Providers) are linked by an assortment of cables owned by others e.g. telephone companies, and anyone with a computer can dial into the network and access information held on it.

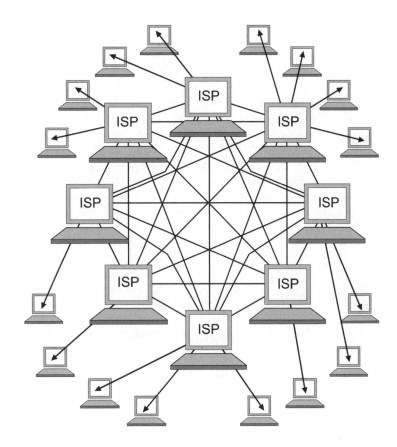

The connection between the end user's computer and the ISP's server need only be a local phone call away, yet the user can access information from the other side of the world which may be routed through more than one server.

How did it start?

Surprisingly the origins of what we now call the Internet date back to the early 1960's and like so much of our modern microelectronics, its roots lie in war, not peace.

During the late fifties the Cold War was at its height and America and Russia wanted to know what each other was doing. The US Defence Department formed ARPA – the Advanced Research Projects Administration.

The Internet's roots lie in war, not peace.

ARPA recognised that an information system comprising a central super-computer controlling a network of smaller computers would soon become top of the enemy's list of strategic targets. And if it were destroyed, the entire system would fail. ARPA conceived and developed an information network which could not be felled in a single blow. Their solution was not to have a central server but to spread the control over several servers so that whichever servers were knocked out by the enemy, the rest of the system would continue to function. Essentially ARPAnet, as it was termed, was the first decentralized computer network and it evolved into what we now call the Internet.

For more information on ARPAnet, visit *http://www.dei.isep. ipp.pt/docs/arpa.html*

Controlling Bodies

The key feature of the Internet is that it doesn't have a core. Just as ARPA conceived a decentralised network to prevent the enemy attacking the key element of the system, we have inherited that legacy and what has stemmed from that is the fact that nobody is in overall charge of the Internet. There are millions of people all over the world who are in charge of their little bit, but their jurisdiction doesn't go beyond their front door. And if anyone decides to close down their bit, hardly anyone will notice the difference.

This, it transpires, is both the Internet's strength and its weakness.

As nobody is in overall charge, it is difficult to apply any legislation to control it or regulate it or determine what information is held on it.

The Internet Society was formed to try to establish and maintain common standards. After this came the Internet Network Information Centre (which registers domain names) and the World Wide Web Consortium which tries to establish future developments, in particular programming languages.

These are the only widely recognised bodies who have any say in how the Internet is run and how it is developed. They are the nearest there is to a central authority, but in reality, nobody has the last word.

Nobody is in overall charge of the Internet.

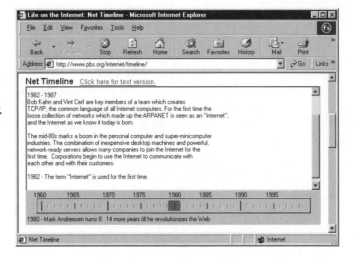

For a full history of the Internet including ARPAnet, there is an excellent timeline at *http://www.pbs.org/internet/timeline/*

Anyone can join the Internet in almost any capacity. Anyone can send messages over the Internet and anyone can publish whatever they want on the World Wide Web. Individuals can even set themselves up as Internet Service Providers, if they have enough financial clout and a modicum of technical knowledge.

Press coverage on the Internet has alternated between hype and hysteria. All the negative features (of which there are several) are reported on over and over again.

Pornography is high on the list, and seems to attract the most consistent coverage. Yet pornography has been available a lot longer than the Internet.

Sites which incite racial hatred have also had their fair share of airtime. There's not much that can be done about them, but if you disagree with their content, don't visit them. If you're worried that you might accidentally stumble across them, don't be. It does happen that people accidentally find themselves in an undesirable site, but it is very infrequent.

Don't get too bogged down with the negative aspects of the Web.

The question of illegal material is a difficult one because what is illegal in one country might not be in another. If you think you're likely to be offended, don't go there.

Sites which provoke public disquiet also feature in the news quite regularly, although not always directly. A recent car cruise in Slough, England was publicised over the Internet. Young drivers with high performance cars gathered to race and show-off on the public roads. What they didn't take into account was the fact that the Police also have access to the same Internet resources and so over 90 officers turned up to greet them.

Stories are now coming to light about drug dealers emailing school children. Doubtless there are other stories in the background waiting to surface.

So why should anyone want to be associated with this filth and degradation?

It is important to balance the negative aspects with the undoubted benefits. People should be aware of the pitfalls and take appropriate measures to protect themselves and enjoy the Internet for what it is – a learning resource, which can and should be enjoyed by everyone.

What do you need?

This chapter outlines what you will require to get connected and offers some alternatives to get you online as painlessly as possible.

Covers

Chapter Two

The hi-tech shopping list

To get yourself connected to the Internet, you need the following:

- a computer

- a modem

- a phone line

- an internet account

- a browser

The Computer

Although theoretically almost any computer will do, in practice you need a reasonably fast one, especially if you want to be able to use all the multimedia bits. Modern websites contain all manner of goodies such as sound, graphics and even animations and video clips, so you need a computer which will be able to download and run these.

The easiest way to increase the speed of a PC is usually to add more memory.

The current minimum specification is a computer with 32Mb (megabytes) of memory and at least a Pentium 1 processor or equivalent, although if you are buying a computer now you should look for at least 64Mb of memory (to enable you to do things other than use the Internet) and you'll probably now only be able to buy Pentium III or the equivalent, as the Pentium II processor is just about obsolete.

You also need a good screen. Certainly one capable of supporting SVGA graphics. Until fairly recently computers were supplied with 14" monitors. These should not be considered any longer. Go for 15" or, if you can afford it, and have the space for it, 17" monitors are becoming more widely available.

If you suffer from headaches, a TFT screen might be beneficial.

The latest generation monitors are TFT screens similar to those used on laptop computers. They offer numerous benefits including virtually no flicker, high resolution and no radiation. They also don't attract the dust like conventional cathode ray tube (CRT) monitors.

The downside is that at about 5-6 times the cost of a CRT monitor of equivalent size, TFT screens are very expensive.

You'll also need a keyboard and mouse (or equivalent pointing device) which means you'll need an operating system which supports a mouse. That means you'll need a PC running Windows 95, or preferably Windows 98 or the networking equivalent, Windows NT4. Older versions of Windows (3.1 or Windows for Workgroups) will work, but you would be well advised to upgrade. All Apple Mac computers qualify, although you should use at least System 7, and preferably a later operating system.

Always try to upgrade to the latest operating system.

To install the software you'll probably need a CD ROM drive as most providers distribute their software on CD ROM. You'll also need some hard disc space to store the software.

Other computers

Most computers used to connect to the Internet are desktop models. But there are two alternatives...

On a direct cost comparison, laptops do not have the specification of desktops.

Laptop computers are perfectly adequate in principle, as long as they satisfy the minimum requirements in terms of memory and speed. The advantage of a laptop is that the screen will be of the TFT type rather than CRT, but the resolution of some older models frequently leaves much to be desired. Screen size is also smaller. Hard disks also tend to be smaller (both in terms of storage capacity and physical size) but that should not be an issue.

Palmtop computers – including the Windows CE models, the Palm Pilot hand-held organisers and most Psion models – can connect to the Internet and there are even sites that have been specially designed with palmtops in mind. Avoid palmtops that do not have touch screens as navigating through the Internet with the cursor keys (the arrow keys) can be frustrating in the extreme.

The major advantage with laptops and palmtops is that they are portable which means you can access the Internet whilst away from your desk.

Laptop computers, sometimes referred
to as Notebooks, can be used to
access the Internet 'on the move'

The Modem

A MOdulator DEModulator is a device that converts the
digital signals generated by a computer into analogue signals
that can be sent down the phone line. It also converts the
incoming analogue signals to digital signals that can be read
by the computer.

*You don't need
a modem if you
have a digital
phone line.*

For desktop computers opinion is divided as to whether an
internal modem is better or worse than an external modem.
For what it's worth, an external modem requires a mains
socket to provide it with power whereas an internal modem
collects its power from within the computer. With all the
other bits and pieces you've got to plug into the mains, the
introduction of a mains-powered modem might be one too
many.

The external modem will also have to be plugged into the
computer and frequently the sockets on the back of many
computers are in short supply. Internal modems, on the

...cont'd

If you have an ISDN phone line, you'll use a device called a router rather than a modem.

other hand, require an internal connection and these are usually in even shorter supply.

External modems provide a nice array of pretty lights to tell you what they're doing, but the case usually looks unsightly (one was once described as looking like a cheap domestic intercom) and it takes up desk space, which is also at a premium.

External modems will work with most computers whether they be desktop, laptop or palmtop. You will probably need to buy any leads that are 'non-standard' and modems that work from batteries as well as the mains are desirable if you intend accessing email away from the office

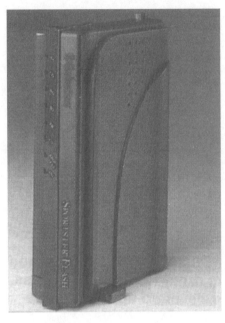

What is certain though is that you should try to get the fastest model you can and at present that is a 56K modem. It may also be advertised as being V90 standard. This is the one to get because it will provide noticeably faster access than anything else.

Fitting an internal modem to a laptop should be left to the experts.

Laptop computers sometimes have modems built into them and are usually top spec. If you haven't got an internal modem fitted, the manufacturer may be able to install one for you. The alternative is a PCMCIA modem which is about the size of a credit card and slots into the side of the laptop computer. There are several types available including ones which will connect to a mobile phone.

Connecting a generic modem to a palmtop can be a daunting prospect. If you're not sure, don't try it.

Palmtop computers usually have modems either built-in or available as an after sales accessory. Broadly there are two ways to add a modem. The first is to buy an external modem specifically designed for your palmtop, the second is to buy a generic desktop modem (preferably with optional battery power to maintain its portability) and the appropriate cables to get the modem and palmtop connected.

A third option available to some computers (notably Psion) is to buy a PCMCIA adaptor which connects to the palmtop into which you connect a credit card modem used on laptops. If you've already got a PCMCIA modem, this is a good option.

Two alternatives

Rather than using a computer and modem, there are a couple of alternatives which could be considered.

This method doesn't require a computer.

The first is an Internet 'set-top box'. These were set to hit the shops in 1998 but some manufacturers couldn't get the price down low enough to compete with the ever-falling price of PCs. NTL are now offering Internet TV as a complete package. A set-top box, as the name implies, sits on the top of your television set. It connects into your television and a suitable telephone point and provides instant access to the Internet.

NTL also provides a remote control QWERTY keyboard as part of the offer.

For more information about Internet TV and set-top boxes visit NTL at *http://www.ntl.com/*

Games consoles

In late 1999, Sega announced a new Internet-capable games machine. Following on from the success of their previous games console, the Dreamcast has a built-in modem so that you can access the Internet. The kit includes a lead to connect it to a phone point and a CD ROM containing Internet access software.

An infrared QWERTY keyboard is available at extra cost, but this would be an absolute requirement if you were considering using the console for email or online chat.

If you want a simple and straightforward solution, a set-top box could be the answer.

With both the games console and the set top box, much of the uncertainty about Internet connection has been removed. You won't need to decide what sort of modem you need, because it's already provided. You don't need to worry about the power of the computer or the amount of memory because that has also been taken care of. In short, what you get is a 'plug-in and go' solution.

But there are some issues that need to be considered before choosing this route. First, all you're getting with the set-top box is Internet connectivity. You won't have a solution that can be used to any great extent off-line. You won't have, for example, powerful word processing or spreadsheet facilities. With the games console, at least you've got a games machine to use when you're not online.

There are sets which will double as a TV and monitor.

The second point is that you will be relying on a domestic television set to view Internet pages, which frequently contain quite a lot of small print. Whilst TVs are very good for watching TV, they're not always very good for viewing pages of text. The alternative is to buy a computer monitor which will improve the text display, but may not be as good for watching TV. Furthermore, the cost of a monitor added to the cost of the set-top box makes it a less attractive proposition.

The phone line

For the desktop computer, you'll need a BT type phone socket near to the computer or a long phone extension lead to connect the modem to the phone line. Kits are available that enable individuals to add a socket to an existing phone installation without having to open the existing phone sockets.

Don't have the phone lead trailing across the floor. Always take it around the edge of a room.

When you are connected to the Internet (online) you are being charged for the call. If you've selected a good Internet Service Provider it will be a local call, but there will be a charge for the call time unless your phone company makes special provisions for going online. The other point to note

Free internet calls are just around the corner. But it will only be to specific ISPs using specific phone connections and at particular times of the week.

is that whilst you're online, the phone is in use. This means that no one can make a call from the phone, and anyone calling you will find the line is engaged.

The cheapest solution to part of this problem is to ask your phone company to provide you with an answerphone service that enables callers to leave messages if your line is engaged. But to really overcome this problem (if indeed it is a problem) a second phone line is required. Many phone companies offer very attractive deals for second lines.

Most phone lines are analogue but digital lines are becoming more common in homes. The price for installing and maintaining an ISDN (Integrated Services Digital Network) line is now much more affordable, and is getting cheaper. The advantage of a digital line is very much faster Internet access, as well as the ability to handle more than one call at a time.

Connecting to the Internet via a mobile phone is a sure recipe for extremely high phone bills.

As to portable computers, you can of course connect them to a land line in exactly the same way as for a desktop computer, but you can also buy kits which will connect to a mobile phone. Strictly these are not modems but adaptors (a modem converts digital signals to analogue but a mobile phone, being digital, does not require an analogue signal).

Satellite Connection

If you really want to set the world on fire, or you consider ISDN too slow or too outdated, then why not try using a satellite connection. Kits to connect to a satellite are becoming much more affordable. Basically they comprise a card to plug into your computer which costs about 3 times that of a good quality modem and a monthly subscription charge of about 3 times that of an Internet account. But, you get a connection claimed to be up to 5 times faster than ISDN.

For more details, including checking if a satellite footprint covers your area, visit *http://www.satweb.co.uk/*

Internet accounts

To get to the Internet, you must have an account with an Internet Service Provider (ISP).

A few years ago there were relatively few providers. All of them charged their clients per month and some imposed monthly time limitations. Today there are many more ISPs from some very unlikely sources. Many are free.

With free ISPs, beware of the hidden cost – telephone help can be very expensive.

When choosing an Internet Service provider you should consider eight points...

Questions and answers

1. How much does the connection cost per month?

It varies, but can cost as little as nothing. Don't write off a provider who charges just because they charge. Not all free services offer the quality of those providers who do make a monthly charge. Different providers offer different deals at different prices. You get more or less what you pay for.

2. How much online time are you allowed before the price goes up?

You should have an account with unlimited access. If the one you're considering doesn't have this feature, leave it and go for another.

Some ISPs offer free telephone connection at certain times of the week.

3. Do you connect via a local phone number?

If the connection to the ISP is not via a local phone call (e.g. an 0845 number) you're heading for some very large telephone bills. Discard any ISP which does not use local call connection.

4. *How many people can the ISP support at any one time?*

It is sometimes quite tricky to get hold of this information. Beware of some of the new free services as they often do not have the infrastructure to support huge numbers of people. One famous case occurred quite recently when it came to light that a particular free ISP could only support 1500 people on line at a time. No wonder the system was always busy and nobody could get connected!

Create a table if you really want to compare ISPs seriously.

5. *How fast is the connection?*

Like the previous point, it's not always easy to get the answer and when you do (unlike the previous point) the answer doesn't always mean much. Free ISPs often don't run very fast systems. The result will be slow connections, slow download times, but high phone bills.

6. *Are you charged for online Technical support? If so, how much?*

This is the downside of many free ISPs. Technical support is usually via a premium rate call which works out very expensive. You only need two 10 minute calls per month (which isn't difficult) and you could have spent as much as the most expensive ISP. On the other hand, if you don't call their helpline ever again, you're in profit. (But then, presumably, you wouldn't be reading this book!)

7. *Does the ISP agreement include email? If so, how many addresses?*

Most do include email, but check on the speed of the email delivery as well. Many ISPs provide more than one email address at no extra charge which means you can have a

Multiple email addresses on the same ISP account usually mean everyone can read everyone else's mail.

different address for each member of the family. Be aware though, like the letter box on your front door, all emails fall onto the same 'doormat' regardless of who it is for. Emails don't come in envelopes though, so privacy could be an issue.

8.   *Do you get space on the ISP's server to publish your own website? If so, how much space and how much will it cost?*

Most ISPs offer space to publish your own website. Some of the free services charge for this, whilst the services that charge per month throw this in as part of the deal. Don't be fooled into going for a huge amount of webspace. Most ISPs offer 5Mb which is more than enough to publish even the most comprehensive family website.

These eight points are, to a large extent, intertwined, but they are worth investigating very carefully.

Where do I start looking?

Some of the leading subscription ISPs are...

AOL	—	http://www.aol.com
BT Internet	—	http://www.btinternet.com
Cable & Wireless	—	http://www.cwnet.com
Demon	—	http://www.demon.net
Direct Connection	—	http://www.dircon.net
Easy Net	—	http://www.easynet.co.uk
Global Internet	—	http://www.global.net.uk
MSN	—	http://www.msn.com
Onyx	—	http://www.onyxnet.co.uk
Virgin net	—	http://www.virgin.com

The free ISPs are provided on CD ROMs which can be freely picked up in many stores including...

Freeserve	—	Dixons, The Link, PC World
In 2 Home	—	Electronics Boutique
Zoom	—	Burtons, Dorothy Perkins, Evans, Topshop, Racing Green
Breathe net	—	Toys 'R' Us
Current Bun	—	Comet
btclick.com	—	British Telecom
freebeeb.net	—	BBC TV

Other free Internet services are available from Woolworths, Nationwide and WH Smith, to name but a few.

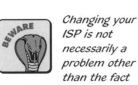

Changing your ISP is not necessarily a problem other than the fact that it will also mean your email address and website address will change.

Once you've selected an ISP and received the installation disc (which will usually be on CD ROM, although some may offer a choice of floppy disc installation), follow the instructions carefully.

Browsers

The browser is the program that essentially does two things. Firstly it is the software which enables the user to commute to different websites throughout the world. Secondly, it displays the pages of information from the websites.

In simple terms, the browser decodes documents written in a special language called HTML (Hypertext Markup Language). There was a stage when websites featured phrases like 'best viewed with Netscape Navigator', because the different browsers handled documents in very slightly different ways causing slight differences in detail.

If you specifically want Internet Explorer, use an ISP that provides it.

Of all the browsers produced since the Internet first became widely used, two have established themselves as supreme: Internet Explorer and Netscape Navigator (latterly tied up in the total Internet package called Communicator).

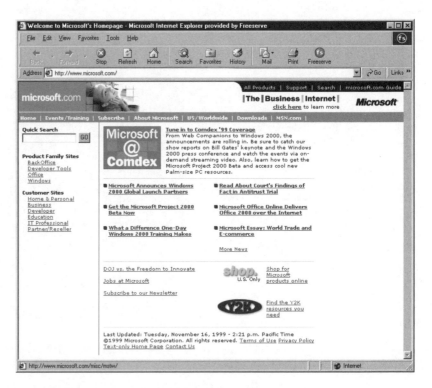

Microsoft's Internet Explorer

Microsoft's Internet Explorer is now just about ahead of Netscape, largely because (some would say) it is supplied free with all versions of Windows. If you've got Windows, you've got Internet Explorer. Further, if you receive a free Internet start-up kit, the chances are it is supplied with Internet Explorer, not Netscape Navigator.

If you specifically want Netscape, use an ISP that provides it.

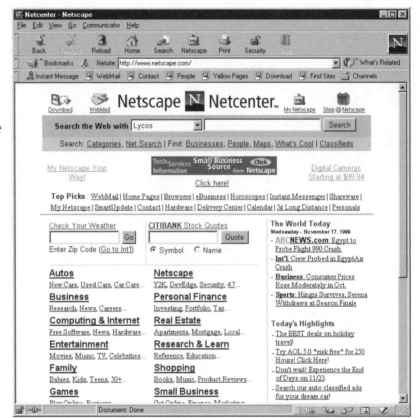

Netscape Navigator

New versions of both programs come from Microsoft and Netscape at regular intervals. It's usually worth getting the latest version which will invariably contain the latest gizmos.

Which browser should I use?

Unless you have decided that you want a particular browser, then it'll probably be best if you stick to the one provided by your chosen Internet Service Provider. Of the discs provided by ISPs for free Internet access, most include Internet Explorer and that will be the browser that will automatically install.

Some 'experts' will try to persuade you that one is better than another, but when they are challenged to provide reasons for their choice, the arguments frequently don't hold water. In fact, in most cases, the explanations provided are based on blind prejudice rather than any logical reasoning.

Stick with the browser supplied by your ISP.

Views along the lines of 'Anything to do with Bill Gates can't be good' are typical of the explanations forwarded by Netscape followers, whilst Explorer fans will say that there is less chance of their browser conflicting with other Microsoft products.

The reality is that there isn't much to choose between either of them. Each time a new version of either package is released it leapfrogs the opposition. So at the moment Explorer may be technically more advanced in some small area, Netscape will then bring out an upgrade that will overtake Explorer, then a new version of Explorer will overtake that and so on.

There are two pieces of advice worth noting when choosing a browser.

1. Whichever browser you choose, make it either Netscape or Explorer unless you really know what you're doing and don't mind being in a minority with a browser that will almost certainly not have had the significant investment of time and money (over a substantial period of time) for its development.

2. Stick with your choice. It's not worth swapping back and forth between them. You can just about run both side by side, but it is not recommended.

Getting it going

Having got all the bits together, what do you need to do to get it going, and what do you do when it goes wrong? This chapter explains all.

Covers

Chapter Three

Install and Connect

It's not easy to give a complete and foolproof description of how to set up the Internet software because currently there are 100s of ISPs offering different products that each install in slightly different ways. Generally, following the on-screen instructions should work.

The example here is using the WH Smith Online disc which is fairly typical of the free ISPs.

If you've activated the Windows Web style feature (Start, Settings, Folder Options), instead of double-clicking (here and elsewhere in this chapter), you should single-click where appropriate.

1 Start up your computer and insert the ISP's CD ROM into your CD ROM drive.

2 It should start automatically, but if it doesn't, go to My Computer and double-click on the CD ROM drive (usually Drive D).

3 You should then get the startup logo with some installation options. Choose full installation.

At this point, some ISPs may ask you to complete a registration form which will include your name, address and telephone number, and possibly some other information like the type of computer you're using.

Read the licence agreement carefully.

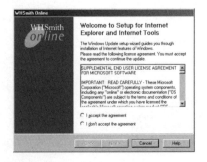

4 Next comes the licence agreement. Read it and if you agree, click I Accept... and then click Next.

5 You will usually be asked to choose which parts you want to install. It's usually best to stick with Typical. (You can always install other bits later on.)

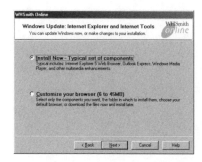

Free Internet CDs are a good way of getting the latest version of your chosen browser.

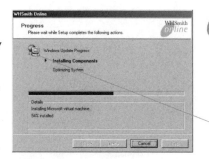

6 After clicking Next, the software will start to install. The blue bar keeps track of its progress. Often there will be a little animated logo which will also help to show that it's all working properly.

7 When the software has finished installing, click on the Finish button and the computer will restart.

This process will have installed the latest version of the browser. Or, to be more accurate, you'll get the version of the browser which is on the installation disc, which will usually be the latest version. If you have a browser already installed, the installation software will only install the browser if it is a later version to the one already installed.

Along with the browser, other software will have been installed. This will vary between different setup discs, but typically you could expect an email program and a Web design program.

When the computer restarts, it will continue with the registration procedure. You will then usually get a licence agreement from the service provider. Again, read it carefully and click OK if you agree with it.

It is usually at about this point that the software tries to dial up for the first time. Make sure...

1   The modem is connected to a telephone socket.

2   Nobody else is using the phone in another part of the house/office.

3   The phone line is actually working.

Click the OK button to register and you should get a dial up status box showing that the computer is trying to dial the number.

Someone else on the phone is usually the reason for a failure.

Some phone companies provide a different dialling tone if you have a message waiting. The alternative tone fools the modem into thinking the line is busy.

When you have successfully connected, you may need to do nothing else, but you may be asked to register your name and address with the ISP.

This will almost certainly be the case if you are using a subscription service, rather than a free service. Typically you will also be given a password with a subscription service.

If you were successful, you should get to your ISP's home page.

If you get a blank page, try typing in the name of a website in the panel at the top.

You will often find a new icon has appeared on the desktop. Double-clicking this will begin the registration procedure. In future you can double-click this icon to get connected.

You'll notice that on the right hand side of the icon bar (bottom right of the screen) there will be an icon showing two linked computers. The screens will flash from time to time indicating that data is flowing between your computer and that of your ISP. Right-clicking on the icon will open a menu giving you the option to disconnect or open a small window giving details about the connection. The window will give you an indication of the speed of transfer - the higher the better.

What if it goes wrong?

Getting connected to the Internet is not as easy as some would have you believe. It can be an extremely simple task, but it can just as easily be a nightmare.

Troubleshooting

Problems will be either hardware related or software related. Hardware problems are the easiest to sort out so it's often best to start with them.

1.   Is the modem working?

The way to check that the modem and the computer are communicating is to go to Start, Settings, Control Panel and double-click on the modem icon.

1 Click on the Diagnostics tab and select the modem you are using.

2 Click on More info...

3 If this window comes up blank, the modem is not being recognised by the computer. Clearly this will need to be investigated.

2.   Is the modem actually dialling a number?

This can be checked very easily by turning up the volume of the modem so you can hear what it's doing.

Return to the Control Panel and double-click on Modems.

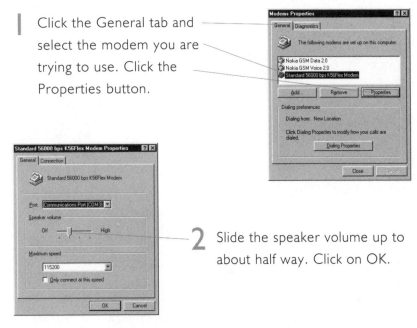

1 Click the General tab and select the modem you are trying to use. Click the Properties button.

2 Slide the speaker volume up to about half way. Click on OK.

If you lift a telephone receiver you should hear lots of screeching.

This should enable you to hear what's going on. When the computer tries to connect, you should hear the dialling tone, then you should hear the tones as it dials and then you should hear a screeching sound as it tries to communicate with the computer at the other end.

If you don't get any sound output, (and assuming the sound on the computer is working) then check the connection between the modem and the telephone socket. If you do get some sound output, but not as previously described, it's probably because...

• the ISP is engaged

• the computer is trying to dial the wrong number, or;

• other details (e.g. password) are wrong

If it's a free ISP, then an engaged signal is not unusual. Try again later. But the fact that you have got some sound output means that it's not a hardware fault, so you need to look at the setup.

If you've followed the set up procedure, the correct phone number should have been automatically inserted, in which case it's unlikely to be wrong unless the ISP has changed its number (which is not unheard of). To check it, open My Computer, and double-click on Dial Up Networking.

You may also double-click on the file in Dial-Up Networking to connect.

1 You should see a file which was created by the installation software. Right-click on it and choose Properties.

2 Check the number is correct. If it isn't, change it and click OK.

Next, try connecting from the Dial-Up Networking file. Right-click on it and choose Connect.

This will open a dialog which should contain the username and password. If the password field is blank, insert your password, click on Save password and then click on Connect.

The computer should try to dial and you'll get a message on the screen telling you that it is dialling.

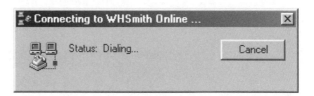

Once it has communicated with the ISP's computer, it should try to verify your password. A message to this effect will be displayed.

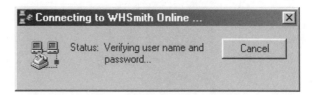

If you've got to this stage, you're almost home because only two things can happen. It can reject your attempt to connect because your logon details are incorrect or it will successfully connect you, in which case you will see...

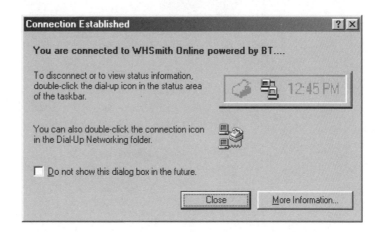

If you get this message, you've succeeded. You're online.

If you've got online by double-clicking the connection file in Dial-Up Networking, you can then start the browser by double-clicking on the browser icon which should be on your desktop.

If launching your browser doesn't get you connected, look at the browser settings.

You should get your ISP's home page. If you don't, but instead get a blank page, try typing in the address of your ISP's site. It will usually be found on the packaging. WH Smith's home page is *http://www.whsmith.co.uk/*

Even if you're not using WH Smith as your ISP, typing in this address should still give the same result.

It's ever so slow

The World Wide Wait, as it is sometimes termed, can be painfully slow. Getting connected can take an age, but once you are connected, getting to a particular website can take so long that your computer gives up. The possible reasons for this could be...

1. You're trying to download a page containing huge pictures. Unless you've got a reasonably fast computer and a very fast modem, some sites are going to be very slow. Website designers generally prefer to use icons for links rather than a simple word which has been entered as text. The benefit is much clearer and slicker sites, but they do take longer to load because a picture, however small it is, uses much more memory than a single word.

2. The ISP you've chosen isn't very fast or isn't capable of handling the traffic. The problem with some of the smaller ISPs is that they simply do not have the network infrastructure to cope with a high volume of traffic. This problem seems to be particularly noticeable with some of the free providers although it certainly does not apply to all of them.

The Internet is sometimes referred to as the Information Super-Highway. If this is the case, some ISPs appear to be connected via a bridle path.

3. The rest of the world is also online. There's not a lot you can do about that other than to try again later. Some people will tell you that the afternoon in the UK is slower because it's the morning in the US and they are getting out of bed and coming online. Others tell you to avoid lunch times as all the kids in school are trying to connect, or Sunday afternoon because that's when the hobbyists like to try. The fact is, wherever you are in the world there will be groups in other parts either at work or play trying to get online.

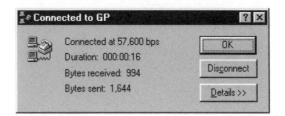

Ping

Another way of checking to see if you have a good connection between your computer and your ISP is to run a program called Ping which is supplied with many setup discs.

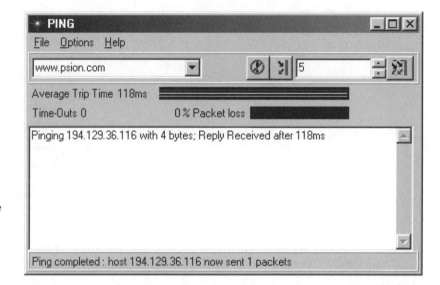

The response should be instant.

This particular program came from the Netscape setup disc. All you need to do is type in the name of a website and click the Ping button. If it is successful your ISP's computer will immediately return a message which will include a number made up from 4 sets of digits separated by full stops.

If you don't get this, but instead get an error message, disconnect and try reconnecting.

The World Wide Web

This chapter introduces you to the World Wide Web, a massive repository of human knowledge. It shows you how to surf the Net, how to find what you're looking for, and how to avoid what you're not looking for.

Covers

Chapter Four

WWW overview

It's remarkable what a catchy name will do. Call it a publications bank (which is effectively what it is) and nobody is interested. Slap on the snazzy tag of World Wide Web, and suddenly everyone wants to know about it and be a part of it.

The Web is simply a part of the Internet, and probably of no greater importance than some of its other parts. The Web is a repository of ideas, jottings, articles, news, research material and general information. Whatever subject you care to name, there is bound to be something about it somewhere on the Web. The trick is finding it.

Even the Queen of England and the President of America have websites.

The rise in popularity of the Web is quite extraordinary. In the early 90's very few people had heard about it. Ten years on and anyone who is anyone not only uses it, but has their own website.

Websites can be published by anyone from the largest corporation to the humblest individual. For example, every car manufacturer worldwide has a website and alongside that school children have their own sites. People publish webpages about their hobbies in the hope that others with similar interests will get in touch. Families have websites, which is a great relief as they seem to have taken over from those endless evenings viewing the neighbours' holiday snaps.

Companies have sprung up specialising in Web design and production. In fact one of the most startling features is the Web's standardisation. Once you have a browser, you can view any Web document from anywhere in the world.

This is a testament to the original conception and design of the Internet – it was more or less correct at the start and because it wasn't driven by profit, there weren't dozens of competitors all trying to get their product in-front.

Getting started

Once you have set up your Internet account, run the browser which will connect you to the Web and will display a Home Page.

Initially the Home Page will almost certainly be that of your Internet Service Provider who takes every opportunity to advertise, especially if it is a free service.

Freeserve's Home Page is a particularly good example of an ISP's Home Page, but you don't have to start each Internet session with the page that your ISP decides upon.

To change the home page in Explorer, first go to the new page you wish to display as the opening page. From the menu, click on Tools and choose Internet options from the menu. Click on the General tab and click on the Use Current button. In Navigator, click on Edit and choose Preferences from the menu. Choose Navigator in the left panel and click on the Use Current Page button. Then click OK.

How to work the Web

The philosophy behind the World Wide Web is simple – use key words in a document to link to other documents. In other words, hypertext. This was the original idea of Tim Berners-Lee, a physicist working at the European Particle Physics Laboratory in Geneva.

On the WWW, the hypertext links can connect documents which may be on different computers and even in different parts of the world. As a user, you don't usually know precisely where the information resides, and you don't need to. It's all quite seamless and painless. That is until you find that the rest of the world is also trying to use the Internet and then it can be very slow (i.e. slow to the point that you think it's stopped working).

Look for the links to other pages, but don't forget the 'back' and 'forward' arrows on the browser's button bar.

How do I recognise a link?

Unless specified otherwise, hypertext links will show up as underlined text, usually in a different colour from the rest of the text. Clicking on the link will take you to another document which should in some way be related to the link you selected.

But it is not just words that can be links. Pictures, tables and diagrams too can be linked to other documents. The pictures can be small icons or logos, or full colour photographs. For this reason, the links have become known as hyperlinks.

Sometimes graphics do not show any obvious signs that they are links. This is because (for example) a thick blue line around an icon would spoil its appearance. But all links reveal themselves when the mouse is moved over them because the mouse pointer changes from a pointer to a hand. The three most common pointers are...

    ⌶   over a piece of copyable text

    ☝   over a hyperlink

    ▹   over nothing in particular.

Consider this page from a well-known website.

Hyperlink

Both the underlined text and the picture of the school are hyperlinks. Clicking the left mouse button when the pointer is over one of these links opens...

... a Web page giving details about the school. But clicking on the hyperlink flagged in the top screenshot...

Back arrow

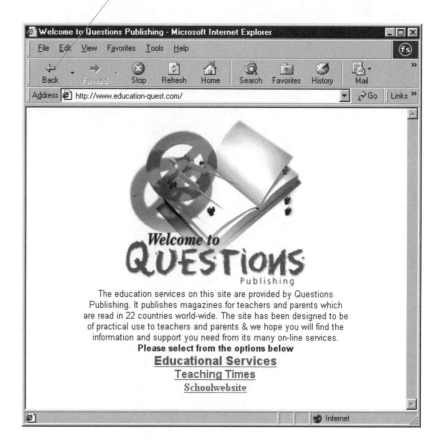

... opens a Web page which is stored on a different computer in another part of the country. In fact, this page could have been stored on a computer in another part of the world.

Once here, there may be links to other sites in other parts of the world.

Don't forget to use the arrow at the top of the browser to backtrack through the sites you visited on route to your destination.

How do I start surfing?

There are several ways to get going, but one of the most straightforward ways is to type in the name of a site in the panel at the top of the browser. The problem with this method is that you have to copy the address exactly as it is written, including punctuation, as one missed full stop will ensure that it won't work.

You can get website addresses from a variety of places. Inclusion of a Web address is now almost obligatory in many forms of advertising, letter heads and business cards.

Once you arrive at a website, there will often be hyperlinks to take you to other related sites. Sometimes the relationship is a little tenuous, but that's the diversity of the Web.

You don't have to enter http:// as most browsers insert it automatically.

In most cases the address will begin...

http://www.

This will be followed by the domain name of the site, which could be the name of a company or individual followed by either *com* or the type of Internet account followed by the country. To be strictly accurate, this would be followed by a forward slash (/) but this can be ignored when typing the address.

Additional slashes followed by other words at the end of an address indicates a page on the website. Therefore...

The second part of this book gives some interesting websites with full descriptions.

http://www.freeserve.co.uk/services

...means that *services* is a page of the *Freeserve* site and typing in that address in full will take you directly to that page rather than going to *Freeserve*'s home page and navigating to the *service* page from there.

Sifting through the Web

The sheer size of the Web is beyond human comprehension. If you want to find a piece of information, or you want to visit a specific site, it is unrealistic to embark on a trawling expedition in the hope that you might stumble across what you want.

You need to organise a search, and for that you need some specialist tools to help you search. Thankfully there are several, and most are free.

There are two main types of search tool that you need to know about in order to find the information you want.

Indexed websites

Sometimes referred to as a directory, this site has been 'hand-built' and contains a hierarchical index. This simply means that a number of subjects are listed as an index. Clicking on one of the subjects takes you to another index listing topics within that subject. Clicking one of those takes you to yet another index of topics. Eventually you should arrive at a list of sites which focus on the very specific subject you're researching.

It's important to remember that indexed sites have been put together by humans and so humans are required to update and amend it. As a result, some of these sites are not always as up-to-date or accurate as one might like.

Search engines

A search engine requires you to enter a word, a group of words or a phrase and the computer (theirs, not yours) will perform a search for that word or phrase. It can search a huge number of pages very rapidly and will (or at least should) return a list of sites that specifically relate to the text you entered.

The trick here is to learn how to enter the word or group of words so that you hit just a few sites, one or more of which, hopefully, will provide you with what you want to know.

It's worth making a search engine or directory your home page.

Searching by subject

The object of any search is to progressively sift out unwanted material.

Searchalot is typical of a number of index sites that can be used to track down information. The advantage of sites such as this is that you can locate the information you need by simply clicking the hyperlinks. The disadvantage is that it will only take you to the home page of each website.

The opening page shows a range of subjects conveniently divided into categories. Every underlined word is a hyperlink so it should be possible to find some information about a subject just by clicking the links.

Each time you click a hypertext link, you'll be taken to another page which only contains links within the subject category requested.

Let's say we want to find some information about Origami (paper folding) and in particular, paper aeroplanes.

Origami is undoubtedly a craft, and in the Art category is a hyperlink called Crafts. Clicking that link opens...

...the 'Recreation: Crafts' page containing links to 2072 sites! Among the topics is 'Origami', and there are links to 60 sites.

Clicking on the 'Origami' link...

...opens the 'Recreation: Crafts: Origami' page with 9 links to sites about paper aeroplanes.

Clicking on this link...

...opens the page which lists the 9 sites about paper aeroplanes. 'Ken Blackburn's Paper Aeroplane' page looks interesting, so click this...

...and up comes a website about paper aeroplanes. On the left is a hyperlink to instructions for making a world record breaking paper plane. Click on this link...

Back arrow

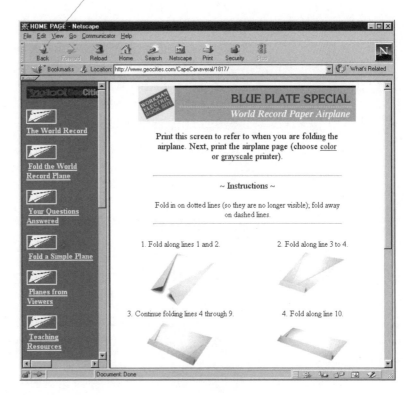

When you get to a site that you think you might like to visit again, save it in Favourites.

... and up come details of the record-breaking plane which you can recreate with the instructions provided in the comfort of your own home.

The flagged arrow at the top of the screen (shown here on Netscape's browser) will take you back to the pages previously visited. This means you can easily backtrack to, say, the page containing the list of paper aeroplane sites and visit another.

A word of caution

Remember, index sites have been constructed by humans and are not necessarily totally accurate. Just because a site is not found using one of these tools doesn't mean it doesn't exist.

Searching by keyword

Another way of searching the Web is to enter a keyword into a search engine.

Search engines work in a different way to an index or directory as the computer tries to match a word or group of words which the user has entered (known as a keyword). The match can be not only against a title of a Web document, but also occurrences of the keywords within the document itself.

There are several search engines which can be accessed either by going to the website of a search engine or by going to another website that uses one of the search engines.

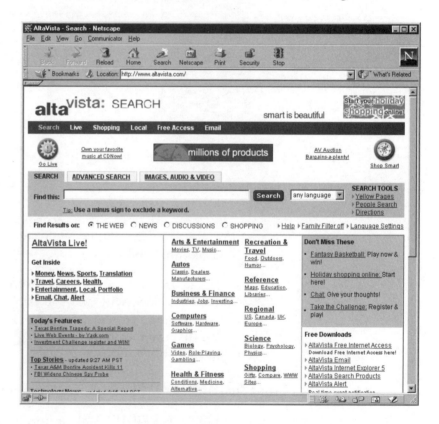

AltaVista is about the largest search engine and can carry out both simple and complex searches very rapidly.

Simple searches

A simple search requires that the user enter a keyword. Continuing on the theme of paper aeroplanes, let's see if there is another way of tracking down the information we're looking for.

AltaVista's home page is at *http://www.altavista.com/*

1 The first task when setting up a search is to choose the language: retrieving unreadable information is pointless. Click on the arrow and choose a language from the menu.

2 Enter keywords in the panel. AltaVista is a particularly efficient search engine which will allow you to enter questions and meaningful phrases as well as a single word. Enter the words *paper aeroplane* and click on Search.

In a few seconds (or minutes depending on the time of day and the speed of your hardware) you'll get the results.

253 articles are returned, which is not bad. (Entering just *paper* or just *aeroplane* probably would have resulted in millions of sites.)

Clicking on the hyperlinks (shown here underlined) takes you to the sites.

But 253 sites are still quite a lot to trawl through so you'll need to narrow it down a little, so that you get fewer results.

The easiest way to do this is to restrict the amount of the Web that is being searched.

Below the AltaVista toolbar is a row of eight buttons called tabs. Clicking one of these will search only in that area of the Web.

Click on the Categories tab whilst keeping the rest of the search setup the same. This search will return...

This restricted search delivers 31 categories on the word paper. About half way down the list is *Paper Aeroplanes* and it shows there are 11 sites on that topic.

Clicking on the link opens the list of sites relating to paper aeroplanes.

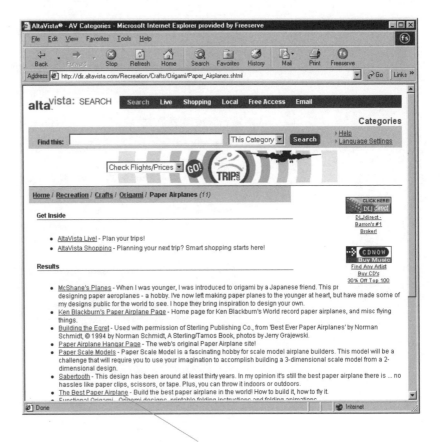

Hyperlinks

Clicking on the hyperlinks will take you to the sites.

Another way to narrow down a simple search is to choose one of the other tabs. Images is often a useful one to use.

Advanced searches

The problem with a simple search is that it often achieves so many matches or hits that you're still left with 1000's of sites to wade through to get the information you want.

Advanced Search tab

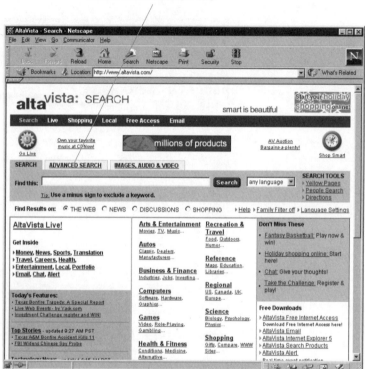

From the AltaVista home page, clicking on the Advanced Search tab opens a page with much more sophisticated searching facilities which should return fewer hits, if you enter the parameters correctly.

When setting up an advanced search, you can enter some additional words which determine how the search engine will treat the keywords you entered. There are about half-a-dozen of these words (known as Boolean operators after George Boole who spent many years studying mathematical logic).

Of the various operators which the search engines understand, the two most important are AND and OR.

paper AND aeroplane

Entering this search will return articles which contain both *paper* and *aeroplane*. Documents that only contain *paper* or only contain *aeroplane* will be ignored.

This is used when you want to search for two subjects that are linked, as is the case here.

paper OR aeroplane

This search will return all documents that contain the words *paper* and *aeroplane*, just as in the previous example. But it will also return all documents which just contain the word *paper* as well as those documents which just contain the word *aeroplane*.

This would be used when (for example) you don't have a preference about spelling. You could use OR if you didn't know whether to search for *aeroplane* or *aeroplanes*.

These operators can be used together to form quite complex statements. Brackets can also be included and these will be calculated first.

paper AND (aeroplane OR aeroplanes)

This expression would search for either spelling of aeroplane and paper. In other words...

paper and *aeroplane*, *paper* and *aeroplanes,* but not *paper* on its own, *aeroplane* on its own or *aeroplanes* on its own.

This is quite different from...

(paper AND aeroplane) OR aeroplanes

This expression (or one similar) would almost certainly be a mistake. It would return documents containing *paper* and *aeroplane* together with all documents containing the word *aeroplanes* on its own.

Once the search expression has been entered, there are some other options which should help to narrow down the results.

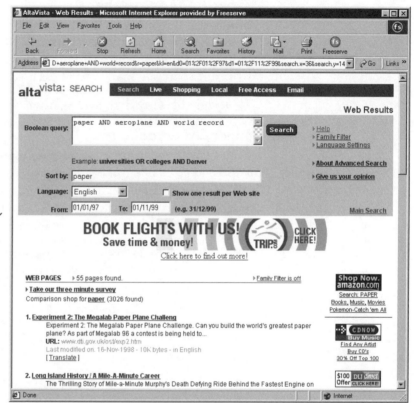

HOT TIP

Ticking Show one result per Web site will help reduce the number of 'hits' on a single site.

As with simple searches, entering the language will remove a large number of documents that you can't read.

If you know the date the document was originally published (or two dates between which the document was published) then you can enter the dates, and documents falling outside those dates will be ignored.

Finding the engines

Experience has shown that rather than needing one search engine, you'll soon find yourself using several. Different search engines frequently give different results for a particular search.

Searchalot provides a simple way of accessing several Internet search engines, enabling you to carry out lots of different searches from the same place.

To select the search engine you wish to use, click on the arrow to the right of the panel headed Search:.

A menu will open (of which this is just a part) listing several search engines. Click on the one you wish to use and its name will appear in the panel.

Now enter a keyword in the panel on the right, and click the Search button to begin the search.

Advanced searches using most search engines can be carried out directly from the Searchalot site, and from many other similar sites.

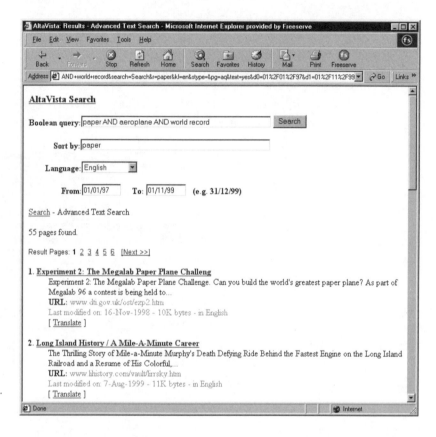

Although not as graphically pleasing as AltaVista's site, this advanced search returns (unsurprisingly) exactly the same results.

Specialist searching

There are sites which offer very specific search facilities within a specific topic. If you want to search for books or music, for example, Amazon is without doubt the best place to go.

When you arrive at the site you can look at stories and articles which can be accessed by clicking the hyperlinks or you can perform a search for a specific book.

1 Choose a book or music from the list

2 Enter a keyword which can be title, publisher or author

3 Click Go

Amazon allows you to enter either the name of an author, the name of a book or a book's ISBN.

Entering *longitude* displays the books with 'longitude' in the title, but also displays other books which might be on the same or similar subjects.

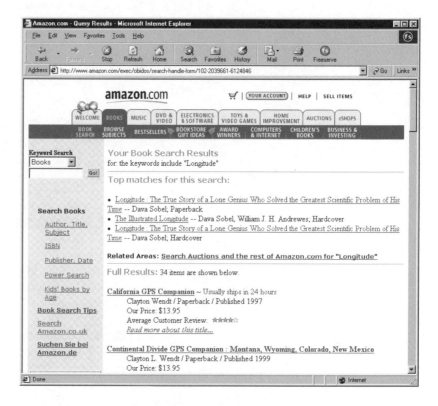

This is a simple search facility which can generate a large list of books. If you know the name of the author you can enter it but it will not necessarily list only the books by the author you chose. It almost certainly will list some books by authors with a similar name.

Clicking on the name of the author will search for other books by the same author. Again, it's searching for a particular word. Any other author with the same name will also be included in the final list.

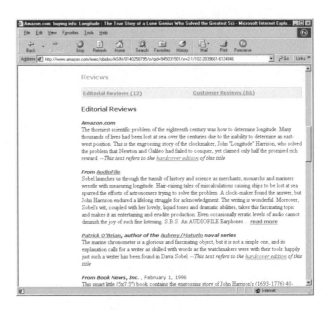

Look out for special offers like signed copies of books.

Clicking on the name of a book will display information about that particular book – usually in the form of a third party review, or as above, two third party reviews.

Clicking on the name of a book will again display information about the book, frequently with a picture of the book cover.

Yellow Pages

Now you don't have to 'let your fingers do the walking' because Yellow Pages are on the Web and are far, far easier to use than the book version.

Go to the Yellow Pages home page at *http://www.yell.co .uk/* or *http://www.yell.com/* and to start a search do the following:

1 Enter either the type of service or the name of a company or tradesman.

2 Enter the area, which can be either a place or a postcode.

 This is far easier than using the book version.

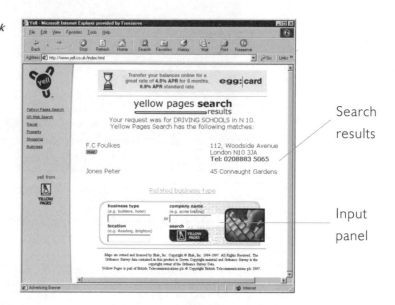

Search results

Input panel

The results come back very quickly and, as can be seen, there are two driving instructors in the N10 area. If the map icon appears alongside, clicking on it will display a map giving directions of how to get there.

The input panel is displayed, ready for a new search.

Webrings

Searching for a specific subject on the Web is not always easy and searching for several sites on the same subject can sometimes be laborious. A clever way of accessing several websites on the same subject is to go to a Webring.

Use your browser's 'Favourites' feature to store useful pages from the ring.

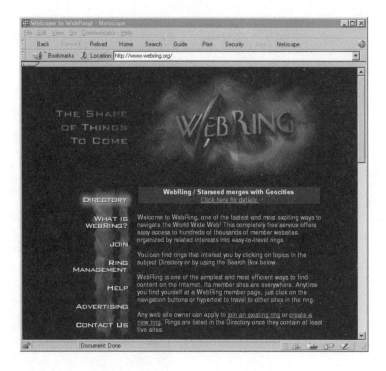

A Webring is a group of websites linked to each other in a sort of circle.

On each Webring website are links to take you either forward or back around the Webring. If you keep going in one direction you'll eventually get back to where you started.

This Psioneer Web Ring site belongs to Geoff Preston
[Site -2 | Site -1 | Random Site | Site +1 | Site +2 | Site +5]
Want to join the ring? Find out how.

Finding a ring

There are two ways to find a webring. The first is to go to the index and choose from the list (categorised by subjects and then topics within those subjects). Clicking on the hyperlinks will take you to a site on that ring.

There is a webring for just about every subject imaginable.

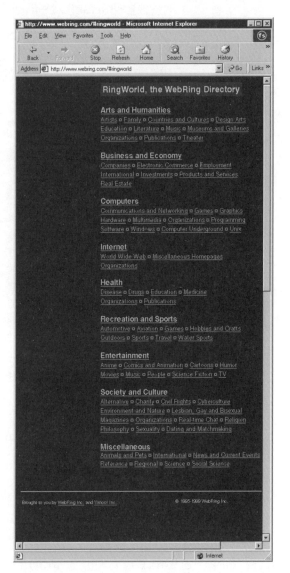

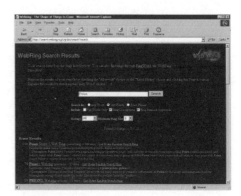

The other way to find a ring on a specific topic is to use the Webring database search. Typing in a word of phrase will list all the rings on that topic.

Anyone can add a site to a ring.

Entering the keyword *Psion* results in 21 rings about various aspects of Psion computers. Clicking on one of the rings (*Psioneer*) reveals 180 sites in this ring alone!

The list of sites is displayed and clicking on one of the hyperlinks takes you to that particular site. Once there, the first thing to do is find the ring icon so that you can navigate around the ring.

Anyone can add their own website to a Webring and details of how to do this may be found on the Webring homepage.

There are hundreds of Webrings on a huge variety of topics ranging from the obscure to the widely popular which can be accessed from *http://www.webring.org/*

Protecting yourself

The Internet is a great tool for kids to learn from. But it does contain some areas that you may not wish your child to visit, and indeed might not want to visit yourself.

The responsibility, in this instance, is firmly with parents. It is wholly inappropriate to buy the kids a computer, install it in their bedroom and then abdicate all responsibility for it. The computer needs to be in a place where its use can be monitored.

Monitoring can be carried out in two ways. First, the occasional glance at the screen. If the screen is in view of parents when a child is using the computer, then all it takes is a quick glance occasionally. In fact, not even a glance is required because if the children know that what is on the screen can be seen by mum and dad, then clearly they're not going to go in search of unsuitable material.

The second method is slightly more devious. Go to the browser and click on the History button. This will list all the sites visited over a given period.

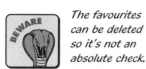

The favourites can be deleted so it's not an absolute check.

You can also get to this list by going to My Documents and clicking on drive C. Open the folder called Windows and inside will be a folder called History. Inside are folders containing the sites visited over a period of time.

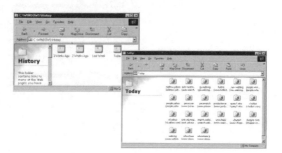

...cont'd

Software monitoring

Parental monitoring is fine provided you are able to monitor the computer's use on a 24 hour basis. Clearly this is not always possible and so you might want to invest in some software protection which will also trap sites found accidentally, and may even limit Internet access.

Net Nanny is one of a number of software tools that will allow parents to control their children's Internet activity by preventing the display of sexually explicit material, graphically violent material, material advocating hate groups and material advocating illegal activity, such as drug use, bomb making, or underage drinking and gambling.

Get Net Wise

Parents can find out more about protecting themselves and their children by visiting *http://www.getnetwise.org/*

There are reviews about a wide variety of children-friendly materials including search engines for kids.

If the kids are using the Internet, a protection program must be regarded as a minimum requirement.

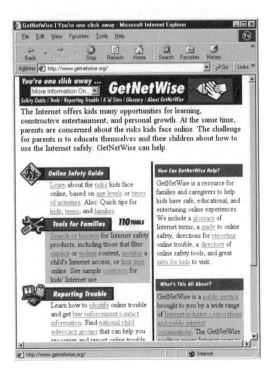

Free speech?

Without doubt, there is a great deal of material which many people would describe as undesirable. In some countries, a great deal of this material is illegal.

Should we protect ourselves from material such as this?

Regardless of which country you live in, the chances are you are living in a free country which supports free speech. It means that we as individuals have the right to say what we want (within certain limits).

Overt searches for pornographic material may be seen as acceptable for some, by some. But surely allowing children to accidentally stumble across this type of material is unacceptable.

If you think you're going to be offended, don't visit the site.

Most newspaper shops sell magazines which would be described as soft-porn. They can be found on the top shelf and although the covers explicitly tell of their contents, they are in fact fairly inoffensive in themselves – usually featuring a scantily clad model which is not much different from what could be seen on any seaside beach. We all know what's inside and if you're likely to be offended, don't open it. This prevents the subject being inflicted on those who do not wish to be part of it, but it's clearly available for those who do. The choice is yours.

In many cases the Internet does not provide that safeguard. Apparently innocent searches can be made but results may include sites of this type which are not presented in a 'plain inoffensive wrapper'. This seems to be forcing the views of one person onto another which is contrary to the principle of free speech.

And what about some of the extreme political parties? Should these be barred? If so, why? Would you want them banned because you personally do not approve of their philosophies? In which case, would you want to ban the websites of any of the mainstream political parties because you also don't approve of their policies?

It's food for thought, nothing more.

Email

This chapter introduces electronic mail and outlines how to use it, and how not to abuse it.

Covers

Chapter Five

What is email?

Of all the features provided by the Internet, this is probably the most widely used.

The world has known about electronic mail (or email) for several years, but it is only relatively recently that it has taken off and become widely known and widely used. Indeed many people would now claim that without email, at best they would be seriously hampered in trying to carry out their daily work and at worst they would simply not be able to function. Frankly I believe the worst-case scenario is a myth – we could function without email, but life is certainly a great deal easier with email than without.

Email is very fast. Send an email and the recipient could get it within seconds, wherever they may be in the world.

The benefits of email are many, but top of the list is probably the fact that recipients can read their mail even if they're away from their desk. The recipient, using any computer in the world (with a phone line attached), can connect to the Internet and any messages will be delivered to the computer that that person is currently using, wherever it may be.

Emailed messages will wait until the recipient is ready to collect them. Messages go into the mail box (which is usually at the recipient's Internet Service Provider) until the recipient logs on and it is delivered.

You can be sure that if you send an email to an individual, that individual will get it, providing s/he logs on to collect it.

The other advantage is that machine readable documents, including (small) computer programs can be attached to emails thus enabling the recipient to amend and print top copies within minutes of the documents being sent.

On the downside, email could all but replace conventional mail with subsequent impact on postal jobs throughout the world. But it is unlikely to completely replace the conventional postal service which can deliver goods as well as the printed word.

You can send email to one person (in which case only that person will be able to read it) or to a group of people.

1 The sender composes a message and connects to his/her service provider. The message is then sent to the ISP's computer.

2 The sender's ISP uses the recipient's email address to pass the message...

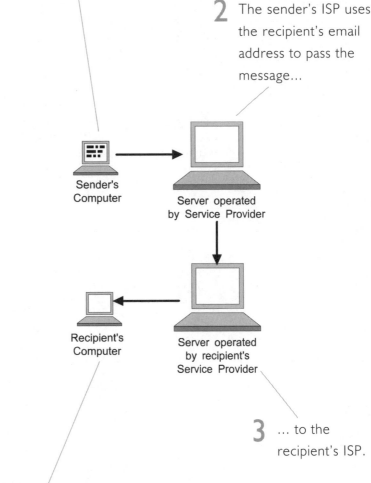

Sender's Computer

Server operated by Service Provider

You may attach a document or documents to an email. For example, you may send a brief message, but attach a ten page, fully formatted MS Word document.

Recipient's Computer

Server operated by recipient's Service Provider

3 ... to the recipient's ISP.

4 When the recipient connects to his/her ISP, the message is transferred to his/her computer.

Email addressing

Generally only lower case letters are used.

Just as traditional letters must be correctly addressed, so too must email messages. Email addresses look confusing, but they are really quite straightforward. The basic format of an email address is...

<user's name>@<domain>.<account type>.<country>

The user's name is that of the individual and would normally reflect the user's real name. (I have three email accounts: *gp*, *gpreston* and *geoff* which I use for different purposes.)

The domain name is the name of the server or service provider on which the account is held. In some cases, this can be changed so that the domain name reflects the name of your company or even your own name.

In this context, the term 'account' does not necessarily imply a financial agreement.

After the domain comes the type of account, then the country of origin, unless the previous part is *com*.

Consider the following account name, which is fairly typical...

gp@freeserve.co.uk

gp	the individual user's name
@	pronounced 'at'
freeserve	the Internet domain
co	indicates a commercial company
uk	indicates the account is held in the UK.

If you're using a computer with a non-standard keyboard, make sure you know how to access the '@' symbol.

For those still confused, a useful analogy is with a conventional address in a street. The name is rather like the name or number of a house. In general, you can have any name you like as long as nobody else in the street has the same name or number. The Internet domain name is like the name of the street. The country is the same. The analogy breaks down a little with the type of account, but it would be rather like putting 'hotel', 'shop' or 'private residence' in the postal address.

The different types of account you're likely to come across are...

ac	an academic institution
com	a commercial company
co	a commercial company
gov	a government department
org	a non-profit-making organisation
sch	a school

The different countries you're likely to meet are...

at	Austria
au	Australia
ca	Canada
ch	Switzerland
es	Spain
fi	Finland
fr	France
de	Denmark
ie	Ireland
il	Israel
is	Iceland
it	Italy
jp	Japan
kr	Korea
nl	Netherlands
nz	New Zealand
se	Sweden
tw	Taiwan
uk	United Kingdom
za	South Africa

It's worth knowing where email addresses reside if only for an indication as to the language spoken by the recipient.

Email software

Managing emails

In order to compose, send, receive and read emails, it's best to have a dedicated program, although you can often access your emails from your ISP's website.

Dedicated email programs usually offer more comprehensive management of your email. There are several to choose from, including many which are free.

The two most common are...

Outlook Express

Although this is given away, it doesn't mean you are free to make illegal copies, or break the copyright agreement.

This email program is usually installed as part of Microsoft's Internet Explorer and as such it's effectively free. It's probably the most widely used email program as it's also the one that's given with most free Internet CDs.

There are four 'trays' for incoming mail, outgoing mail, old messages you've sent and old messages received.

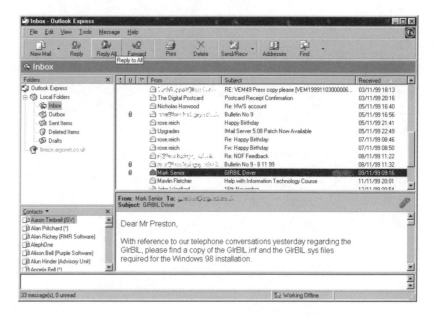

Messages can be easily viewed by clicking on the title of the message (in the top panel) and the contents will be revealed in the lower panel. Double-clicking displays the message in a separate window from where it can be printed.

Netscape Messenger

This comes as part of the Netscape suite and is effectively the head-to-head rival of Outlook Express.

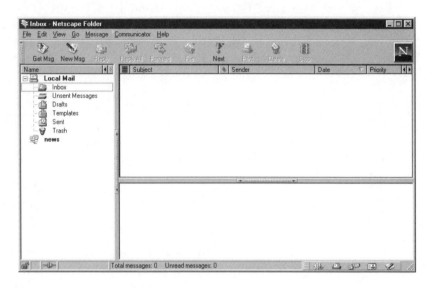

It's not usually worth changing your email program, but it is worth keeping up to date with the latest versions.

The reality is that these two programs are virtually identical (in so far as what they do). In other words, if you've already got one, it's unlikely to be worth your while changing to the other. The additional benefits are unlikely to be worth the hassle of changing.

Others

These are by no means the only email programs available. If you want something different, try Eudora which can be downloaded from...

http://www.qualcomm.com/

There are two versions, 'lite' which is free, and 'Pro' for which there is a small charge but you get several additional features.

Pegasus is available as a free download from...

http://www.cuslm.ca/pegasus/

This is brilliantly simple to set up and use.

Setting up your email program

Many Internet Service Providers (including all of the free ones) supply a disc which will install and set up most of your email account for you. But whatever ISP and email program you choose to use, you'll need to do some setting up yourself. This actually involves little more than entering a few names in boxes. Most of the details will be provided by your ISP, but some details (those personal to you) may have to be decided upon by you.

Your name – when sending an email, your name (which may be your real name, or the name you wish others to identify you by) will be sent along with your messages so that others will know who the message is from.

Email address – if you have been provided with an email address then this will need to be entered so that recipients will know who to reply to.

Incoming mail server – your ISP will provide you with this name but in most cases (where Internet access is via a single computer connected to a single telephone line) the address will be...

pop.<isp name>.<account type>

You will be asked if you want the system to remember your password. If you're the only person using the computer, confirm that you do.

Outgoing mail server – again, your ISP will provide you with this name which will usually be...

smtp.<isp name>.<account type>

Account name – this will be the name by which the account is registered by the ISP. It may or may not reflect your own name.

Password – this may or may not be provided by the ISP. In any event, when it is entered it will be displayed as a row of asterisks so that nobody else can read it.

News server – you may also be asked to enter the name of the news server. Typically, this will take the form of...

news.<isp name>.<account type>

...cont'd

Outlook Express

To change or view your account details in Outlook Express...

I Click on Tools. In the pull-down menu, choose Accounts...

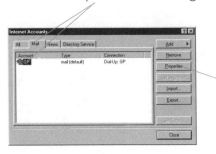

If you want to create a new account, click on Add before step 2.

2 Click on the Mail tab and select the account you wish to change.

3 Click on Properties.

4 The details will be under the General and Servers tabs.

5 Click OK to save any alterations.

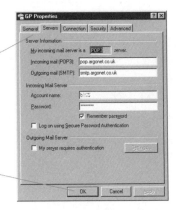

Netscape Messenger

When changing your account details in Messenger...

1 Click on Edit, and from the
menu choose Preferences...

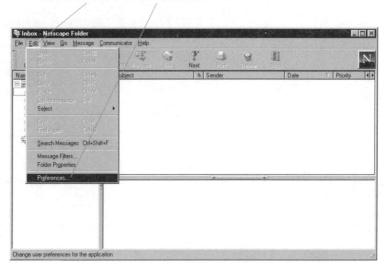

*Several of the
installation CDs
will do this for
you.*

2 Choose Identity and Mailservers to
view or alter the account details.

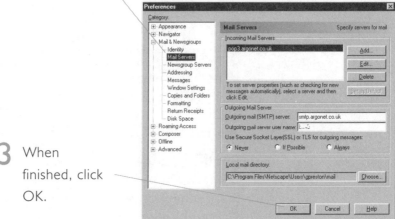

3 When
finished, click
OK.

Fine tuning

Most email programs will allow you to set an assortment of options which will control the way the email program works.

From Outlook Express go to Tools and choose Options, from Messenger go to Edit and choose Preferences.

(Outlook Express)

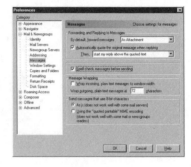

(Netscape Messenger)

You will find the best options for you as you begin using emails on a regular basis, but some of the options you should consider are...

When to connect

You can set your email program to automatically connect as soon as it is started. This means that any new messages will be delivered when you start.

When to disconnect

I can't think of a good reason why you need to stay connected after you've sent and received emails. Set it to automatically log off after send and receive.

Spell-checking

It's worth setting it so that it will spell-check your messages before they are sent. You can also include checking any text written by someone else that is being included in the reply.

Free email accounts

Email need not cost anything, apart from the cost of your ISP and phone calls. If your ISP does not provide a very good email service, or you simply want another email address, try using a free email service like Hotmail.

Log on to Hotmail at *http://www.hotmail.com/*

If you haven't registered, you'll be asked to provide a username and a password. This can be a little tricky as there are several million account holders worldwide, and so choosing a suitable name that isn't already in use is often harder than one would think.

This is also a way of sending anonymous emails.

Once you are registered, you can go to the Hotmail site and enter your username and password.

This, of course, can be done from any computer in the world, so you can collect email when you're away from the office and even using someone else's computer.

When you've successfully logged on, you will be presented with a window listing all the emails currently waiting for you.

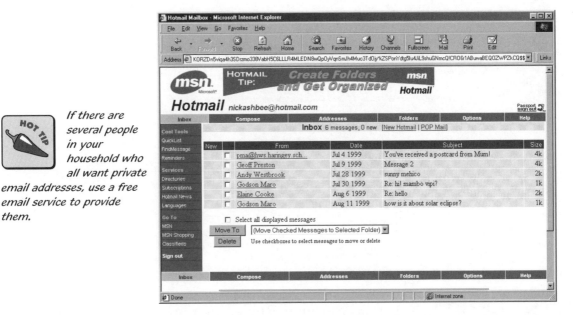

If there are several people in your household who all want private email addresses, use a free email service to provide them.

Those messages which have been read can be saved (to be read again later), printed or deleted. New, unread messages are highlighted enabling you to distinguish new mail from old.

It's far better to compose emails offline.

You can create new messages in Hotmail although it's sometimes better to prepare messages in a word processor whilst 'offline' and then copy and paste the text into the Hotmail editor when you are online. This practice reduces the phone bill very significantly.

Apart from a recent blip in the system when some hackers found their way in, Hotmail is a very secure service, and very fast.

Web mail

Accessing emails from your ISP's website

Many Internet Service Providers offer their customers the facility of accessing their emails directly from their website.

Argonet is typical. To access your email from their website...

Go to their website and look for the link to take you to your email.

This is the best way to access your email if you're trying to do it away from your computer – at an Internet Cafe for example.

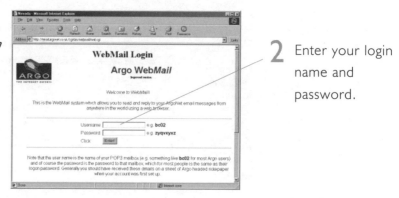

2 Enter your login name and password.

This opens your email account showing what emails you have, which are new and which have been read.

If you're going away but still want to be able to access your emails, remember to take your login name and password with you.

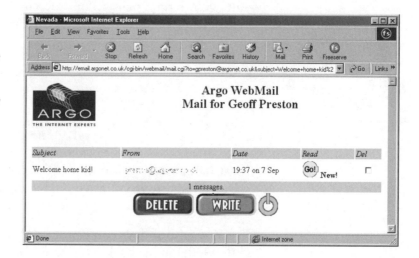

Corporate email

Many companies run an internal mailing system which works in exactly the same way as Internet email, but some mail is kept within the company.

Typical of the many programs used for this is IMail which enables users to send both corporate and Internet email. Users create mailings and, depending on how they are addressed, IMail will determine where they go. A full email address will be sent via the Internet, whereas anything less will be sent internally.

Your loved one might not appreciate you taking your work on holiday.

IMail offers the user several additional features which could prove invaluable. You can tell the system to redirect the mail you usually collect via IMail to another (Internet) email address. This means that you can collect your corporate mail when you're away from the office.

If you're on holiday, you can tell IMail to send an acknowledgement back to anyone who sends you an email telling them you're away and you'll reply when you return.

Anatomy of an email

Address books

The trouble with most email addresses is that they are anything but memorable. Some are little more than an apparently meaningless string of characters – sometimes not even containing letters in the first part.

Some email programs can be set up to automatically add names from all incoming and outgoing emails to the address book.

Most popular email programs have an address book which enables you to store the names and addresses of those you frequently contact. Using this system, you can simply enter the person's name in the To box, or even just select it from a list.

The added advantage is that when you look at emails you have previously sent, you can quickly see who you sent them to.

You can also send to several people by creating a list in the To box.

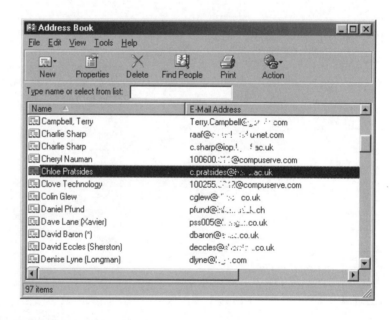

CC and BCC

When you've selected the recipient you may, if you wish, forward the email to another person by entering another recipient in the CC or Counter (Carbon) Copy box. If you don't want the recipients to know who else you have sent the message to, you should put the other names in the BCC or Blind Counter (Carbon) Copy box.

Subject

It's worth including a short phrase in the Subject box as it gives the recipient an idea of what the message is about before they open and read it. It is particularly helpful if, like me, you store past emails for reference. If there's a subject, you can quickly scan the messages for the one you want. If you find you've got 20 messages from the same person and none contain an indication of what they are about, it could take a long time to find what you're looking for.

The body of an email

An emailed communication can seem a little curt (rather like a telegram) and some people can be offended by this. It is particularly noticeable if a reply contains huge chunks of the original mailing with just a couple of words added.

A whole new writing style has developed with emails.

To be on the safe side, especially when sending an email to someone for the first time, lay it out a little like a traditional handwritten letter. Begin with 'Dear' and finish with 'Yours'. (Don't bother to include your address at the top right!)

If they reply in a more relaxed manner, then you can follow suit if you wish.

An email can say a lot about you – just as a letter can.

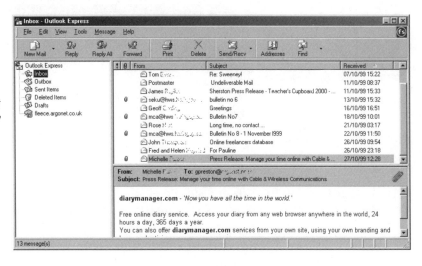

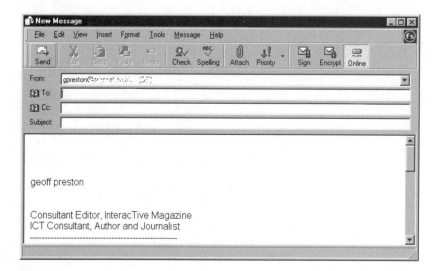

If your email program cannot automatically append a signature, try creating a signature as a text document and pasting the contents into your mailings.

Signature

Many email programs allow you to automatically append your own signature, comprising anything from your name to contact telephone numbers and even cute philosophical messages. But care should be taken not to overdo this feature. For some people, email is a serious means of communication and half a page of gibberish about your views on the meaning of life together with an extended list of ways you can be contacted may not be deemed very time-friendly. It's also not always appropriate to inflict your own musings on others.

A further development on this theme is to build up a sort of picture using keyboard characters, and include that as part of your signature. Usually the backward and forward slash ('/' and '\'), the 'greater than' and 'less than' signs ('<' and '>') and an assortment of other characters like 'O' and 'o' make up these works of art.

They can, of course, say a great deal about the sender. Personally, when I receive an email with one of these at the foot, I usually think, 'This person is paid too much for doing too little' or 'What a twit!'.

Sending an email

1 Open your email program and choose the New Message icon:

(Outlook Express)

(Netscape Messenger)

2 This will open a window into which you compose your message.

3 Enter the email address of the recipient...

The upper window is from Outlook Express, the lower from Netscape Messenger.

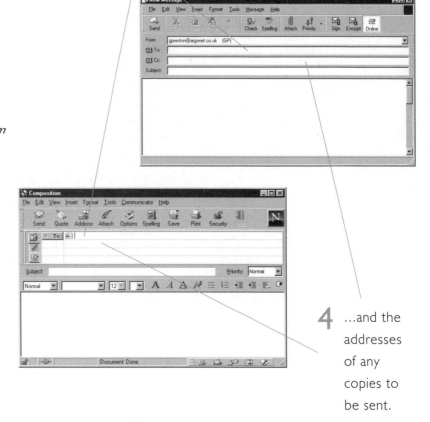

4 ...and the addresses of any copies to be sent.

5 Click in the Subject panel and type in a brief phrase for the subject.

6 Click in the main window and type your message.

7 When your message in complete, click the icon to place the message in the Out tray.

(Outlook Express)   (Netscape Messenger)

If you are currently connected to the Internet, your message can be sent immediately, but will not be sent until Send/ Receive is clicked. If you're not currently connected, your message will remain in the Outbox until you next log on or click the Send/Receive button.

Replying to emails

The most popular way of replying to an email is to simply return the received mailing with your own notes added. If one applies that approach to traditionally written letters, it would be considered inappropriate, to say the very least. Yet, email programs actually encourage this approach by offering the user the opportunity of automatically including the original text when replying.

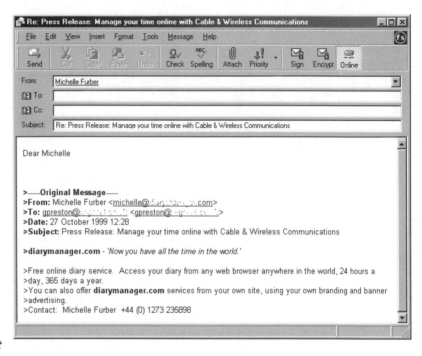

Some recipients don't like having their email returned with just a 5-word response tagged onto the bottom.

When an email arrives which requires a response, choose Reply and a new email will be generated with the recipient's name and email address included. The text from the original message will also be included but each line will be prefixed with a mark (usually '>') to denote that it has been copied from the original message. Your reply can be placed before or after the message to which you are replying, or better still, intermingled with it. For example, if the sender has made several points that each need to be addressed as a separate issue, then it's best to put your response with each point.

Forwarding an email

Received emails can easily be 'bounced' to someone else – a practice which is becoming more popular. But do beware. Sometimes emails arrive which are for you and you alone and not for sharing with the world at large. Remember, if you send an email to someone else, they can send it to another person who in turn could send it to someone else.

 If you don't want an email forwarded, put a notice at the bottom to the effect that this is a private message and is not to be forwarded.

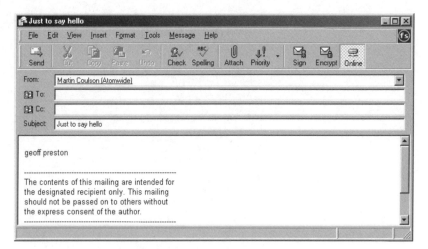

There are some occasions when an email is sent with the specific intention of passing it on to as many people as possible – virus warnings for example. If you receive a notification of a possible virus, forward it to everyone on your mailing list, even if you think it might be a hoax.

Returned email

If you incorrectly address the envelope of a traditional letter, it's unlikely to get to its intended destination. With email it's more certain – it definitely won't get there. It will simply be returned to you as undeliverable. You'll probably get a computer-generated message from a postmaster somewhere telling you it was undeliverable. The original text will usually be included with the message. Check the address and re-send.

Who has an email address?

The actual number of people who own an email address is estimated to be about 20,000,000 worldwide. The number of people who use email regularly is more difficult to establish. But the reality is that everyone probably knows someone who has an email address. You can find email addresses from the Internet by going to a site that maintains an email address database. Typical are *www.whowhere.lycos.com/* and *www.hotbot.com/*

Whilst you're on this site, why don't you enter your own email address so others can find you?

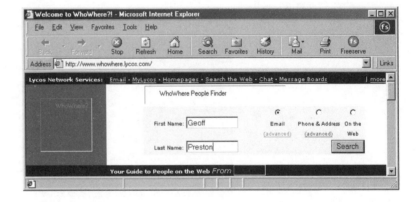

Once you've arrived at the site, enter the first name and surname of the person you're trying to contact. You'll probably get several people with the same or similar names, but you should be able to locate the right one.

Clicking on the email address will create a new email document addressed to the correct person.

Sending documents

In days gone by, sending files along with your emails was a long and involved process. Now, with more modern software, attaching documents is simply a case of dragging and dropping. The necessary encrypting and decoding is all done automatically in the background.

Don't try sending very large documents. It's really annoying when you try to collect your email and find it takes an age because someone has sent you a 5 Mb file.

Pictures, word-processed documents and spreadsheets can all be sent as an email attachment. The recipient receives the document which can be opened immediately or saved.

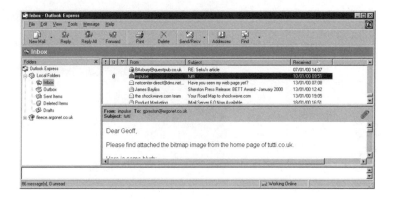

When an email is received which contains an attached file, the first thing you'll notice is that the download time is increased. Different email programs show attachments in different ways. (Outlook Express displays a paper clip symbol.)

Attachments are notorious for containing viruses – especially if the attachment was created in MS Word which can store viruses in macros.

Opening the mail or clicking on the symbol reveals the attachment. Double-click on it to open it or save it to disc.

Compressing and decompressing.

If you want to send an attached file with your email, it's often best to archive (or compress) it first, especially if it contains pictures. One of the most popular compression programs for PCs is WinZip which can be  downloaded from *http://www.winzip.com/*. For Mac users, try StuffIt which is available from *http://www.stuffit.com/*

 The recipient needs to have the same program to decompress the attachment.

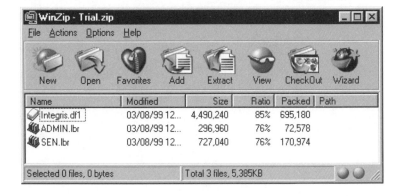

 Many email systems automatically place a limit on the size of the mailing. Hotmail, for example, has a 2 Mb ceiling on emails.
Anything above this size will be rejected.

WinZip and StuffIt will compress files and folders very efficiently so they occupy a lot less space and consequently can be sent considerably faster. But you should still watch the size of the file you are sending.

When you receive attachments they may be compressed in which case you'll usually need WinZip or StuffIt to decompress them before they can be read.

Sometimes people send a self-extracting file which simply means that, when you've downloaded it and saved it onto your local hard disc, double-clicking on the file will cause it to decompress itself without the need for a program like WinZip.

Beware when receiving attachments. Make sure you have a good virus protection program running before you attempt to open them. Even so, treat unsolicited mailings with attachments, especially from unknown sources, with extreme suspicion.

Secure delivery

Unlike handwritten and hand-signed letters, it is difficult to prove that an email came from a particular individual. Emails are now frequently used to send confidential material, where letters in sealed envelopes were previously used.

Digital IDs ensure that emailed documents are not forged and that the person who reads it is the intended recipient and nobody else. It is the equivalent of sending a letter in a sealed envelope and requiring the recipient to sign for it on delivery. You can even encrypt the message using a digital ID.

A digital ID comprises...

• a public key

• a private key

• a digital signature

To digitally sign an email, you add your digital signature and a public key to the message. This is known as a certificate.

Getting a Digital ID

1 In Outlook Express, go to Tools and select Accounts.

2 Choose the account in which you wish to have a Digital ID and click Properties.

3 Click on the Security tab...

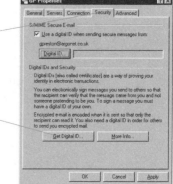

4 ... and choose Get Digital ID.

This will open a website which will allow you to choose Verisign – one of the largest providers of Digital IDs.

For a small annual fee they will provide everything required for a Digital ID, including details about setting it up and using it.

If you intend sending confidential material, always use a digital signature.

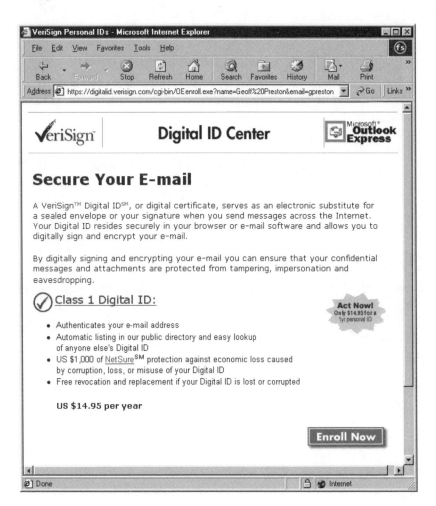

Better emails

Well, not better, but different. Emails tend to look very plain and bland – rather like a telegram. Just as people send less than formal letters on fancy paper, so too can you send your social emails with a designer backdrop.

Rather than simply clicking on the New Message button in Outlook Express, click on Messages on the menu bar and choose New Message Using. This opens a sub-menu which allows you to choose different stationery for your email.

Some of the styles might not be your first choice for, say, a job application.

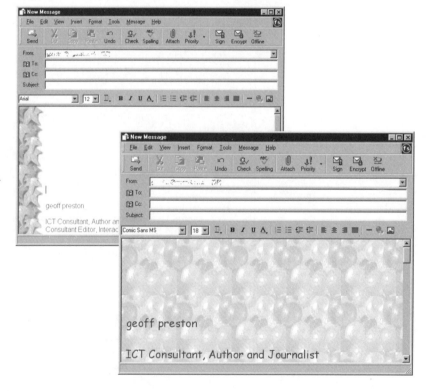

The various styles include different backgrounds, different font styles and sometimes different font colours. Quite a change from the usual black on white.

Greetings

This is a lovely idea that can really brighten someone's day. Rather than sending a plain email, send an electronic greeting.

There are dozens of sites that offer this free service, amongst them is ICQ who are at *http://www.icq.com/greetings/* Most require the same sequence to be carried out, although there are some variations between the different sites.

This is a great way to brighten up a loved one's day.

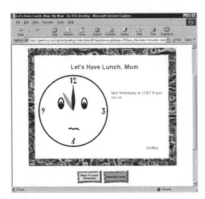

When you arrive at the site you'll need to choose a category. There are dozens to choose from ranging from passing a driving test to religious festivals.

Once you've selected the category of greeting, you need to select a card. These range from tasteful to less than tasteful, but there's something for everyone, including cards with music and movies.

You enter your name and email address, and then the name and email address of the recipient. Finally, send it.

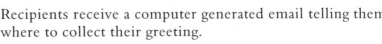

Recipients receive a computer generated email telling them where to collect their greeting.

Abusing the system

Just as the Internet is used for doubtful purposes, so too is email. And it's virtually impossible to bring the culprits to book because free mail services like Hotmail are anonymous and therefore virtually untraceable.

Incoming mail

In schools, this can be a serious problem. All students at a particular school will have similar email addresses. Once you know the common part it's fairly easy to get to the rest so individual students can easily be contacted. Stories abound about drug deals cooked up via school-based email services.

It's very difficult to track down the authors of inappropriate emails.

It's difficult to police because the contents of mailboxes can't always easily be accessed by others (including the network manager and the postmaster). Even if they could be accessed, trawling through hundreds, if not thousands of mailings looking for suspicious contents is not a practical proposition, even if the messages have been saved on the system.

Outgoing mail

The other problem is with inappropriate messages leaving your email account or email domain. If others use your email account or domain, there is a danger of them using the system for all manner of purposes that you may not like. Again, this is difficult to police, especially in an institution with hundreds of users.

Some email programs allow the system supervisor to create a short warning message which will be automatically tagged onto every mailing. If users know that a warning along the lines of, *'If you are offended by the contents of this mailing, please return it to...'* is automatically sent out with every email, they will usually refrain from sending anything likely to cause offence.

But, to put it into perspective, if a person wishes to send inappropriate material, they can do it with traditional letters. Email just means they don't have to walk to the postbox.

Email annoyances

A whole new culture has developed around the use of email. This development has accelerated noticeably during the last three or four years when computers have become much more widely available and are now being sold with Internet connectivity built-in.

Built-in Internet connectivity means, by definition, built-in email as part of the computer package on sale in the same shop that sells washing machines and hi-fi. When you buy a washing machine, you get a manual telling you how to wash clothes. When you buy a computer you don't get a manual telling you how to use email.

Regrettably many people find themselves with email included in their new computer package but don't really know how to handle it properly. For them it's a hobby. For others it is more serious.

If you don't want an email forwarded, put a notice at the bottom to the effect that this is a private message and is not to be forwarded.

In the order of my own personal annoyance...

1. There is a growing assumption that emails should be replied to immediately, or at least within the hour. Some people seem to think that your life involves little more than sitting in front of the computer waiting for emails to roll in. If you don't respond immediately they send another complaining that you haven't responded to the first. The very nature of email encourages this desire for immediate action and reaction. Previously, a letter would be handwritten and taken to the postbox. A reminder would not have been sent until (usually) at least a week had passed. Be patient, do not expect an instant reply, even though emails are delivered more or less instantly.

    However, that said, it's worth having a standard reply message that you can quickly send which basically says you've received an email and you will respond to it in due course.

2. Recipients seem to think it's acceptable to distribute your mail to whoever they see fit. This should not be

done unless you are specifically invited to do so. A friend of mine sent an email to a group of people and one of them decided to publish it in a local parish magazine without even asking him. (And without even attempting to correct some of the mistakes which are almost inevitable if you're composing an email on a palmtop computer in the middle of Tanzania.)

This practice is not on. After all, you wouldn't consider photocopying a letter you received and distributing it to anyone and everyone.

3. People seem to have trouble knowing how to construct an email. If writing a letter using pen and paper, the normal salutation is *Dear Sir*, *Dear Jill*, or *Dear Revd Barber*. Emails seem to discourage this approach and as a result you get greetings like *Hi Pete*, *Hello*, or no salutation whatsoever. If it's a formal email, be on the safe side and begin *Dear...* If replying to an email, it's probably safest to use the same format as was sent. Although I do draw the line at copying salutations such as *Hi-ya Geoff*, *Watchya Mate* and *Howsitgoin' Sport*.

Smileys

Emails can seem a little aggressive if they're put together too quickly.

To try and lighten them, or to try to ensure the recipient reads the message in the same tone as it was written, some people include 'smiley faces' (sometimes referred to as emoticons) in their messages.

Personally I'd rather receive an email that was written in such a way that the underlying tone could not be misunderstood. (I don't remember ever reading a paper-based letter punctuated with smiley faces.)

Some of the most common are (and these are usually read sideways)...

:-)	I'm happy/pleased
:-D	I'm laughing
:-(	I'm sad/angry/cross
:-|	I have no particular emotion
;-)	I have a raised eyebrow
:-O	I am shocked
:'-(	I am crying
:-*	I am kissing you
:-P	I am sticking out my tongue
:-)>	I've got a beard (actually, I haven't)
8-)	I'm wearing glasses (actually, I'm not)
:-X	I won't say a word

Reading too many of these may make you want to go for a pint of (_)] (not read sideways).

If you feel you need to use one of these, try re-wording your message so you don't need to.

TLAs

AKA (also known as) three-letter acronyms, these result from either laziness or just simply 2M2D (too much to do). They have been used in emails FSY (for several years) and are analogous to, and about as understandable to outsiders as CRS (Cockney Rhyming Slang).

Rather than writing out the whole phrase, it is reduced to its SPA (smallest possible abbreviation) which is a group of (usually) three letters, which ideally SFAW (should form a word) and PSV (preferably something vulgar). WAL (with any luck) the recipient will understand WYM (what you mean) but often they just leave the reader LOL (laughing out loud).

Too many TLAs makes text DTR (difficult to read).

If you find this GR8 (great) explanation is ALC (a little confusing) then you can always RTM (read the manuals) supplied with your computer which could MIC (make it clearer). OTOH (on the other hand) you may decide to GTAM (give them a miss) which is MFS (my favoured solution) as it KMIAJ (keeps me in a job) by STN (sustaining the need) to write books such as these.

BTW (by the way), I try to avoid TLAs largely because I GDU (generally don't use) many stock phrases. IOW (in other words) it is +LY (positively) inappropriate for most of my writings, although I do find myself using them when TDN (taking down notes) on my PDA (personal digital assistant), but not when I'm otherwise ATK (at the keyboard).

I HTH (hope this helps) when GTRM (going to read mail) which is VLP (very liberally punctuated) with meaningless TLAs.

If you fully understood TLAs before reading this CESB (chapter of an easy steps book) then some would suggest you GAL (get a life). Many will have found it useful and would like to CTA (congratulate the author), but NRN (no reply necessary).

OWOW (one word of warning); some of these TLAs are TUB (totally and utterly bogus)!

Newsgroups

This chapter introduces newsgroups and outlines what they are and how you can access them. It goes on to explain how to post your own articles and how to stay out of trouble with the other members of the group.

Covers

Chapter Six

What is a newsgroup?

Many people have tried to explain what a newsgroup is by weaving a witty analogy which invariably gives away the author's feelings on the subject. The truth is that these homespun philosophical gems are, in the main, correct although I've yet to find one that fully explains a newsgroup.

So as not to disappoint, try this one...

A newsgroup is rather like a large receptacle into which you can place any number of pieces of paper containing, questions, an answer to a question, personal feelings, whatever you like.

At any time you can dive into the receptacle, read any of the pieces of paper and if you wish, reply to some of them.

The only restriction is that the contents of each receptacle should be on the same subject. The receptacle is clearly labelled with the name of the subject and although there is nothing to stop you putting in a piece of paper with a question about another totally unrelated subject, there wouldn't be much point because it will probably be discarded.

HOT TIP

If you wish to quote this analogy, replace each occurrence of 'receptacle' for 'filing cabinet' if you approve of newsgroups, or 'dustbin' if you don't.

(If you go to the receptacle expecting to find comments about subject X and you pull out a piece of paper relating to subject Y, you too would probably discard it.)

As the author of a piece of paper that you placed in the wrong receptacle, you might even get a lecture about what the receptacle is for and where you should have placed your piece of paper.

Certain individuals have seen newsgroups as a route to cheap (i.e. free) advertising.

They go around dumping adverts into the receptacles, usually when you're looking through them, so that they land, not amongst all the other pieces of paper, but on the top so that they're right under your nose.

One more thing: my ISP alone hosts over 32,000 receptacles. Each receptacle can (and frequently does) hold thousands of pieces of paper from all round the world.

Whoever coined the phrase 'information overload' was certainly familiar with newsgroups.

Newsgroups have been referred to as the Internet equivalent of Speaker's Corner in Hyde Park, London where anyone can go and stand on a soap box and pontificate. Newsgroups have also been described as electronic whingeing, hi-tech gossip and computerised scare-mongering.

More positively, they have been described as electronic billboards where people can post articles and others can reply to them.

Newsgroup addressing

The name of a newsgroup provides the description of the subject.

In general terms, the name takes the form...

<type>.<category>.<topic>

For example...

rec.video.production

The type is recreational and the category is video. The topic within that the video category is production.

Some of the most common newsgroup types are...

alt.	Alternative
bionet.	Biological
biz.	Business
comp.	Computer
microsoft.	Support for MS software
misc.	Miscellaneous discussions
news.	Usenet discussions
rec.	Recreational activities
sci.	Scientific discussions
soc.	Social and religious discussion
talk.	Anything controversial

This list doesn't even represent the 'tip of the iceberg'.

Newsgroup types that begin with the name of a country (fr, de, be, es, uk etc.) are subjects of particular interest to nationals of that country and will often be in the language of that country.

What do you need?

If you have Outlook Express or Netscape Messenger then you have everything you need to access newsgroups.

Specifying a News Server

You'll first need to enter the name of your News Server into Outlook Express or Netscape Messenger.

(Outlook Express)

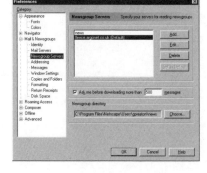

(Netscape Messenger)

Your Internet installation disc may have done this for you.

In Outlook Express go to Tools on the menu bar, open Accounts and click on the News tab. For Netscape Messenger, go to Edit on the menu bar, choose Preferences and click on Newsgroup servers.

You'll then have to enter the name of the News Server which will be provided by your Internet Service Provider.

Typically, the name of the News Server will be along the lines of...

Stick to one server – the one provided by your ISP.

\<name\>.\<isp name\>.com

You can use as many News Servers as you wish, but there's not usually a great deal of point as many of the newsgroups will be duplicated, and even if that were not the case, one news server will provide far more information than one person can possibly cope with. Servers such as Pipex host most of the newsgroups and the only ones they don't host are the 'undesirable' ones.

Downloading the newsgroup list

This can take a considerable amount of time – up to 60 minutes depending on speed of connection and the number of groups hosted by your ISP. Fortunately, this only has to be done once.

(Outlook Express)

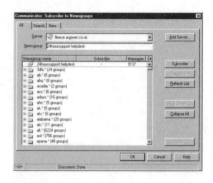

(Netscape Messenger)

The number of newsgroups is staggering. My server hosts over 32,000 but there are probably twice that number worldwide. Some are not very popular, but others (like the newsgroups dedicated to the finer points of Microsoft's Windows) have a huge number of readers.

Registering

When all of the newsgroup names have been downloaded, you can decide which groups you wish to use (or subscribe to). You can add to the list and remove groups from your list as often as you like, but initially you should restrict yourself to just one or two groups which specialise in a subject in which you have at least some knowledge, if not expertise.

Initially register for 1 or 2 groups only. You can always add more later.

To subscribe to a newsgroup, (using either Outlook Express or Netscape Messenger) select the group and click on the Subscribe button. To unsubscribe, click on the Unsubscribe button. A flag will appear at the left showing which groups you are subscribed to. Clicking the button labelled Subscribed or Subscribed Groups will list only those groups you are subscribed to.

Searching for a newsgroup

To make life a little easier, both news readers provide a search facility so that you can quickly find newsgroups within a particular topic. If you enter a name in the search panel, you're sure to find something.

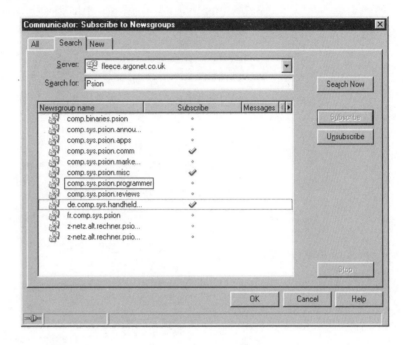

Always use a search rather than trying to wade through the list by hand.

Even topics that one might think are fairly small and specialised can contain several newsgroups, when one might think there wasn't even enough interest to sustain one group.

When you're more familiar with newsgroups, try entering 'magic' or 'music' to get some information about other topics.

A search for *Psion* (the manufacturers of hand-held computers/organisers) for example, reveals 12 newsgroups. Select the one(s) you wish to subscribe to and they will be added to your list of subscribed groups.

Even when you're more familiar with newsgroups, it's unlikely you'll need to subscribe to more than half-a-dozen. Even with half that number, the amount of articles that will be generated will be enormous.

Downloading the news

All of the messages in your registered newsgroups can now be downloaded.

There are two ways of going about this. You can either download the headers only (that is, the titles of each of the articles) or you can download the headers together with articles themselves.

Downloading the headers only takes a very short time, but to read the articles you'll have to go online. If you download the headers and the documents together, it will take considerably longer, but you can then read the documents offline.

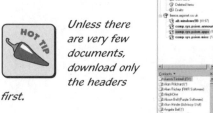

Unless there are very few documents, download only the headers first.

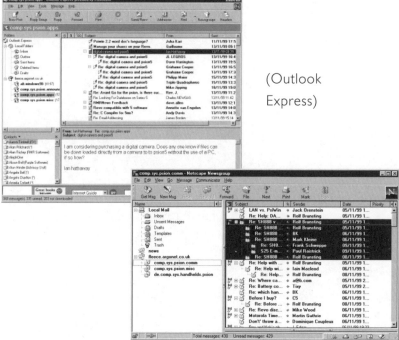

(Outlook Express)

(Netscape Messenger)

The documents are grouped together so that you have the initial document, with the various responses to it. This means that you can follow the discussion even if you joined halfway through it.

Reading an article

If the actual article has not been downloaded with the header then you will need to go online to read it.

With the news reader open so that the headers are listed, you can read any of the articles by simply clicking on one of them to show the text in the panel below the list of headers.

The articles will be grouped so that the original article is on top, and the responses made by others will be immediately underneath. If you see a plus sign alongside a header, clicking on it will show all of the responses relating to the original article. (This can be clearly seen in the screenshots of both Outlook Express and Netscape Messenger on the facing page).

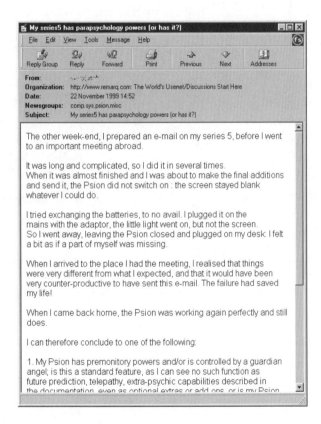

Articles can be about anything from simple questions to bizarre anecdotal jottings.

Alternatively, double-clicking on the header will open the article in a window of its own. You must do this if you wish to print an article.

Responding to an article

After spending some time browsing through the articles and messages that have been placed on the newsgroups, you will almost certainly be drawn in to replying to some. Even if it's only to answer a question to get someone out of a fix.

You can respond either to the group (in which case your response will be added to the list of responses) or you can respond to the originator personally, which is effectively sending an email.

It's more personal if you reply by email.

The Reply Group (Outlook Express) or Reply All (Netscape Messenger) buttons will send your reply to the group. The Reply button will send your reply to the author only.

Either way, type in your reply as you would for an email and click the Send button.

The Reply buttons will send an email reply to the author of the currently displayed message which need not be the author of the original article – in other words, you can reply to one of the replies.

If you can, choose to download only the changes.

Synchronising

New postings to newsgroups arrive very quickly and you'll be able to see your replies almost as soon as you've posted them. You must, however, first refresh the newsgroup's content by clicking on the Synchronise button. This will match all of the headers on your computer with the headers on the server. You should then be able to see your replies (assuming you can find the original article again).

Posting an article

It won't be long before you've been bitten by the bug and want to make your own views known, or feel that this is a suitable forum to try to get answers to some of those burning questions you've been wanting to pose for most of your adult life.

Respond to articles before attempting to post your own. This will give you a better idea of the sort of topics covered by the group.

To post an article, select the newsgroup you wish to use and click on the New Post button.

A window will open looking exactly the same as if it were an email and even carrying your signature (if you set one up for your email).

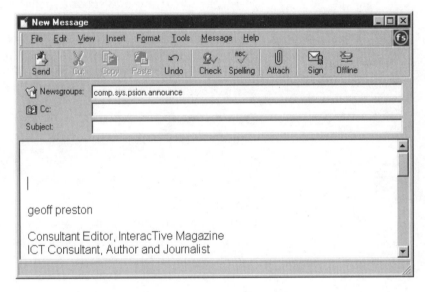

Just as with email, enter your message and send it using the Send button.

Avoid downloading Word documents at all costs – they can contain some hateful viruses hidden within macros.

Attachments

In addition to the textual part of your article, you can also send files including pictures and fully formatted word-processed documents.

Great care should be taken when opening attachments to newsgroup postings as they can contain viruses. In general, only include attachments in the binary (bin.) newsgroups.

Netiquette

Newsgroups have no formal rules, although many have a sort of 'code of conduct' which you are expected to adhere to. The 'rules' can usually be found in FAQ – Frequently Asked Questions. This is known as Netiquette.

The first thing is to ensure you are posting to the correct group – you'll receive a lot of flak if you don't.

Flame wars

Never get involved in a slanging match, known as a flame war. All you'll do is lower yourself to the level of the other person. The trouble is (and this comment will generate a lot of response on the newsgroups) that once someone has sent an email, typed a letter and got to level 2 of the latest video game, they think they're an expert in the field of computing in general (and the Internet in particular) and could have a one-to-one discussion with Bill Gates. You'll never win against people like that, so don't try.

Some newsgroups and newsgroup users have been around for a long time. It's familiar territory for them, but not necessarily for the newcomer.

Don't shout

Capital letters means you're shouting. If you send a message with Caps Lock on, people will think you're being aggressive.

Advertising

Don't post commercial messages in newsgroups. This is called 'spam' and it's not very popular. If you want to advertise, try the business (biz.) groups which were set up for that reason. (The trouble is that nobody ever reads them because they're full of adverts.) But even so, don't post them anywhere else.

If you stick within those boundaries, you're unlikely to fall foul of anyone.

Interaction

This chapter shows you how to communicate with people from around the world using your keyboard to 'talk' and your mouse to 'move'. You can even play board games and card games. Unlike email, this interaction is in real time.

Covers

Chapter Seven

What are chatlines?

Adults should be aware that, like telephone chatlines, these are a constant source of fascination for teenagers.

Although on the face of it, Internet chat seems like a trivial feature, it has its serious uses and has been put to serious use on more than a few occasions.

Since its introduction in the late 1980s, news reporters have used it to transmit accounts of a diverse range of events from the World Cup to the Gulf War.

The reality is that Internet chat is most frequently used as a harmless means of social gossip. A group of people from different cultures and on different sides of the world can communicate with each other in real-time without running up a huge phone bill.

The darker side of this topic is that it can be host to some conversations which at best can only be described as undesirable, punctuated with language which is best described as repetitive.

For the home or school user, chat programs do offer the opportunity to communicate with others from other cultures and have been successfully used to support the teaching of some foreign languages.

There are three main chat techniques available to the user...

If you want to join in, you'll need to be fairly proficient on the keyboard.

*   Webchat

*   Internet Relay Chat

*   Instant messaging

To the casual onlooker, it's actually quite difficult to tell the first two apart. The output is rows of text preceded by the name (or nickname) of the person who wrote it.

The message here is that online chat should be monitored even more closely than Internet use in general. It's a message that I make no apology for repeating.

Webchat

About the easiest way to get started with chatter is to go to Yahoo's chatrooms.

As with all of Yahoo's services, you'll need to register by going to their home page at *http://www.yahoo.com/* (signing up with Yahoo also gives you free access to other Yahoo services). Each time you visit the chat site, you'll have to 'sign-on' by entering your Yahoo ID and your password.

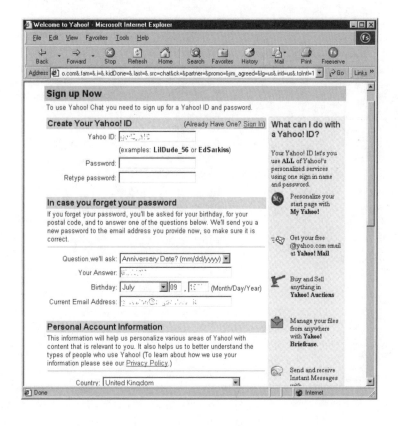

You'll have to register on most of the chat systems. Try to use the same name and password, or keep a note of them all in a text file or database.

Once you've registered, you can start chatting immediately, although you will receive confirmation by email within 24 hours.

Like so many chatlines, Yahoo's is divided into areas called 'rooms'. Entering a chatroom is rather like entering a real room – it may be empty or full, or there may be just a few people present.

Each chatroom is given a name which reflects the topic of conversation you can expect to take part in within that room.

This is a great way to improve your typing skills.

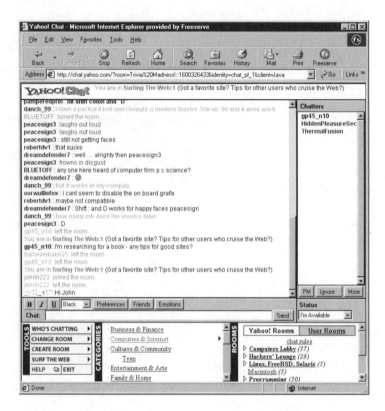

You're unlikely to have a deep and meaningful conversation with an intellectual academic.

You can change chatrooms at any time by clicking the CHANGE ROOM icon at the bottom left of the screen. In the centre panel will be a list of subjects to choose. When you've selected a subject, on the right will be a list of specific topics within that subject. Alongside each topic will be a number telling you how many people are currently in the room. You'll need to find a room that's got more than 1 person, but not dozens or, in some cases, hundreds.

Clicking on the subject will take you into the room where you will be announced as...

<name> has just entered <room>.

The panel just above Tools (labelled Chat:) is your 'mouth'. Type into the panel and press Return to be heard.

Some people take the trouble to colour or embolden their text so that it stands out from the rest.

If children are using this feature, it needs to be very carefully monitored.

Unlike a conventional room, the conversation can be 'heard' by everyone in the room although you can, if you wish, have a private conversation with one of the group. On the right is a list of visitors to the room and right-clicking one of the names enables you to find out more about that person and to have a private chat with them.

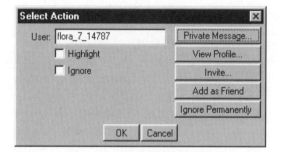

Yahoo chat will also give you access to the so-called Adult rooms. These areas are entered via a warning sign pointing out that you should be 18 to enter. For those who are over 18, enter only if you are not offended. For those over 18 who have children under 18, monitor the use of this chat facility very carefully. This chatline is available to all, it's very easy to register and very easy to access.

Look out also for advertised events in Yahoo's chat rooms. Occasionally they have special guests available who you can talk to. Recent celebrities have included a stress consultant, a dermatologist and a wine expert.

For information about the best webchat rooms, go to *http://www.100bot.com/chat/*

Internet Relay Chat

Internet Relay Chat is rather like the Internet equivalent of CB radio with its own language and customs. It was developed in the late 1980s by Jarkko Oikarinen, a Finnish programmer, and has proved enormously popular.

To use IRC you need to download a small program. If you're using a PC with Windows you need to go to *http://www.mirc.co.uk/*, whilst Apple Macintosh users should go to *http://www.ircle.com/*

The software arrives as a self-extracting file and running it will extract the parts and install it. (These modules are usually shareware which means you get it free for a month after which you have to pay a small fee to keep it going.)

There is a list of commands that really need to be understood before embarking on IRC.

Getting Started

When the software has been installed, run it and the About mIRC window will be displayed which will enable you to register and visit the website should you wish to do so.

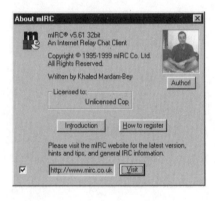

If you're not connected to the Internet, the program will dial your default connection.

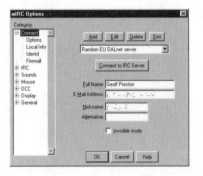

Close the About mIRC window and the mIRC Options window will open which contains your registration details. The only information you need to put here each time is the name you wish to be known by in this session. When you click on the Connect to IRC Server button, you should get online, but if not, try changing the server by selecting another from the list above the Connect to IRC Server button.

You don't use your browser for IRC – it's all done through the downloaded software.

The next window to appear gives you the chance to choose which channel (or room, as it is generally known) to use. At any time during your IRC session you can leave one room and visit another. The rooms are supposed to be named in such a way that the user has at least a clue as to what the topics of conversation are likely be. Unfortunately this is not always the case and finding a suitable place is often a matter of trial and error.

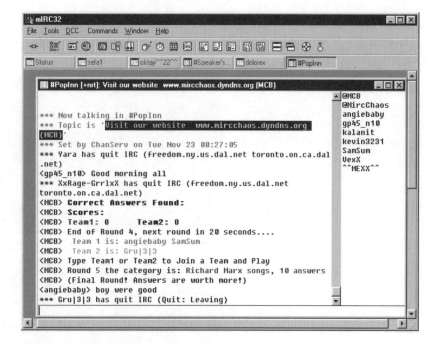

Some people get together and form teams and have a sort of quiz. Right-clicking on one of the names on the right means that you can confer with other team members without the opposition knowing what you're saying.

Instant messaging

Both webchat and IRC are public meeting places that you drop into in the hope that you'll find somebody worth talking to. But even if you do get a good conversation going, others tend to interrupt.

This has led to the development of Instant Messaging or 'buddies' as it is sometimes referred. All the big players have their own version of it (AOL's Instant Messenger, Microsoft's Messenger, etc.) but top of the pile is ICQ (I seek you).

You need to download the program from *http://www.icq .com/* which is available free for a trial period, after which there is a small fee for the licence.

The idea is that you set up a list of contacts (buddies) and when you and they are online, you can 'talk' to each other in private.

This is live, real-time conversation.

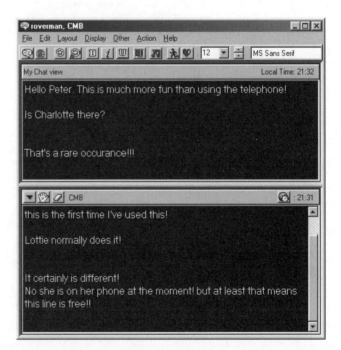

When it's running, you have a window with two areas – one that you type into, and one to display the text your buddy enters.

Once ICQ has been downloaded and installed, you'll need to register after which you will be given an ID number. You'll also need to choose a name which you will be known by. ICQ loads automatically when you switch your computer on and it sits on the Taskbar at the bottom right of the screen. It doesn't do much until you go online when it 'announces' itself to the world at large.

This is a good way of communicating with people overseas without running up a huge telephone bill.

When it's active, the icon changes to a flower, which can also be seen in the ICQ menu, displayed by clicking the icon on the Taskbar.

From time to time, if you're online, you'll get a request to have a chat. The request will pop-up on the screen and contain details of the person requesting the chat. If you agree, the dialogue window will open and you can now chat.

ICQ will announce when one of your buddies comes online, so you'll be able to decide whether to have a chat. Similarly, when you go online, you'll be told which of your buddies is also online.

This can be distracting if you're online as it gives people the opportunity to disrupt you for a chat.

If you get tired of random people trying to strike up a meeting, you can put ICQ into dormant mode which means it's still running, but nobody can see you, although you can still see them.

If you're bored, you can try to set up a chat with someone else. This could be a random chat, or a chat with one of your buddies.

Again, this is real-time chat, but the real fascination is watching the other person typing. The letters come up one at a time as they are being typed. You can even see when they've made a spelling mistake and are trying to correct it.

Interactive games

This is an interesting variation on the theme of chatting.

The Web provides a meeting place for all sorts. If you enjoy playing games, then you can play against others who you will never have seen before, and who possibly hail from the other side of the world.

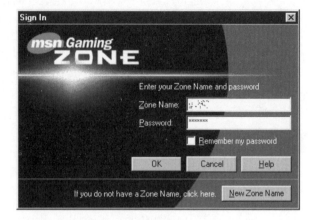

The Gaming Zone is one of the most popular sites for people to chat and play a game at the same time. The site features mainly board games and card games which you play online with others.

When you first visit the site you must register by providing the obligatory username and password. The popularity of this site is such that almost any meaningful username you enter will return a message telling you that that name has already been taken and suggesting half-a-dozen alternatives.

Initially there is a little setting up to do, but it is well worth it.

You'll next have to download some software which takes only a short while but provides you with access to the main areas of the Gaming Zone.

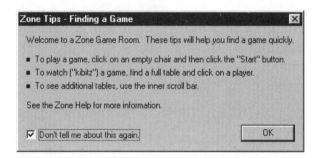

In future, whenever you log on to the Gaming Zone, you will have to enter your username and password.

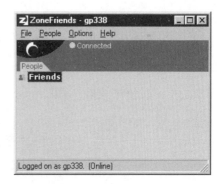

A window will be displayed showing that you are logged on and providing you with some menus which will display your current status.

The options default to leaving you contactable all the time you're online.

You choose a particular game from the list on the first page of the website and when you've made your choice you'll be taken to that particular zone where there are a number of rooms in which people will be playing the game you selected.

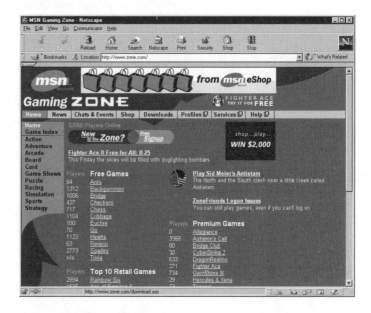

Respect the room levels. If you are a novice, don't go into the room where there are competitions in progress.

When you play a particular type of game for the first time you'll have to download a small module. After that, you will be free to visit any of the rooms in that zone.

Conveniently, each room carries a sign telling the visitor of the likely standard of play within.

Draughts

On entering one of the Draughts rooms (otherwise known as Checkers) you'll find yourself in a virtual room with lots of tables.

If you 'chat' in the room, everyone can 'hear' you.

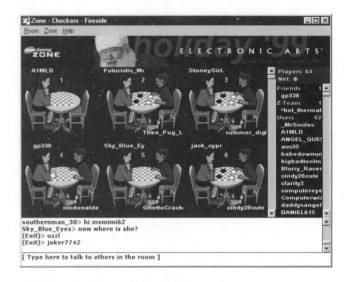

If you see an empty seat, click on it to sit down. If there's someone opposite (and s/he's awake) you'll be invited to play. If you both agree, the game starts. Moves are carried out by dragging the pieces on the board. (You'll see your opponent moving his/her piece.) The computer prevents illegal moves and tells you whose turn it is.

Always introduce yourself to your opponent who may be from another country.

If you wish, you can carry out an online chat with your opponent in the space provided at the bottom of the gaming board.

Bridge

Even more popular than Draughts is Contract Bridge which will involve three others, of whom any or all can be a computer.

You can choose to just watch a game if you wish.

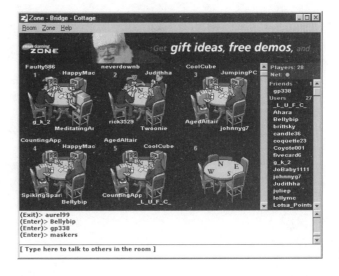

Get to learn the way the site works by visiting and participating in some simpler games first.

As with Draughts, clicking on an empty seat or a seat occupied by a computer will include you in the game. The game of Bridge is much more involved – just like playing the game for real. You will be required to make contracts and you could end up being the dummy hand. If there are not enough humans, the empty seats will be filled by a computer.

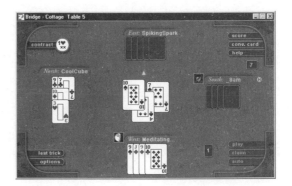

The Gaming Zone is at *http://www.zone.com/*

Graphic chat

A variation on the chat concept is a graphic chatline. It's a sort of cross between a chatline and an adventure game played over the Internet.

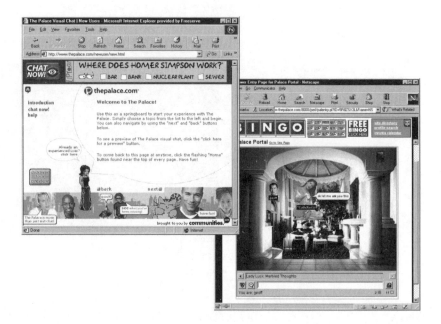

This is addictive.

The Palace is one such site which offers users the chance to visit different locations and chat with the other people there. You can move from one place to another within the chosen location, as well as moving between locations, and searching out interesting people with whom to share your views.

You are given an identity, complete with an icon (which you can change) and what you say appears in speech bubbles, which can also be selected to describe the emphasis or context (saying, thinking, shouting etc.).

If you do decide to try one of these sites, you'll need a fast computer (and connection) as you're downloading some quite large graphics.

To join in, you'll need to download a module which is available from *http://www.thepalace.com/* (The Palace) or *http://www.worldsaway.com/* (Worlds Away).

Virtual reality

Taking this idea still further is Cybertown. This is a virtual reality city which you can become part of.

You enter Cybertown at *http://www.cybertown.com/* and although you can take a limited part in the proceedings, to really get involved you need to register.

The email arrives virtually immediately.

This involves entering a username and a password. Once again, there are several thousand people here and so you'll need to choose something that hasn't already been taken. You must also enter your email address and you will then be issued with an immigration code (password) to allow you into Cybertown.

Once you've registered and logged on you will be given an 'avatar'. This is 'you' in the virtual world and you move your avatar around Cybertown and interact with others.

Cybertown is a 3D world which you become part of, and where you live out your virtual life with others who come and go. Just like real life.

If you know a friend who visits Cybertown, entering their username will get them some bonus points when you register.

Living in Cybertown is not simply a case of roaming around chatting to people you happen to bump into; you really do need to get involved. You'll need, for example to get a job and find somewhere to live. Having said that, you can chat to others; indeed, you need to help each other to a large extent.

This is a game and there is a points scoring system which you need to be aware of. If you can't find anyone to help you, there is a help page which shows you how to buy food, get a job and generally live your virtual life to the full.

Bargains for all?

This chapter shows how the Internet can be used to buy goods and services from the comfort of your own armchair.

Covers

Chapter Eight

The ultimate retail therapy?

Mail order shopping is almost as old as the concept of shopping itself. For years we have posted orders for a huge range of goods which have been advertised in catalogues, magazines or even the morning newspaper. Anything from nails to underwear, from saucepans to armchairs have at some stage been offered by mail order.

In most cases an order form was printed with the advertisement and, when completed by the bargain-hungry customer, was placed in an envelope together with payment (usually a cheque) and sent to the supplier who in return dispatched the goods.

Newspapers still carry lots of mail order adverts.

The stock phrase of the day, *"Please allow 21 days for delivery"*, was because the time taken for the order to arrive by post, for the supplier to process it, package the merchandise and send it off by parcel post, was often that long. Or even longer if demand outstripped supply. Remember, in some cases these orders arrived at the supplier in their thousands. No wonder perishable foods didn't figure very highly in the mail order market.

The advent of credit cards has, to a very large extent, contributed to the more recent popularity of telephone mail ordering. From the retailer's viewpoint, it immediately eliminated the 4 or 5 day wait for cheque clearance. For the customer, quoting a credit card number means that it is no longer necessary to send a letter, as the primary reason for the letter was to deliver payment, which the credit card replaced.

It is now unnecessary to fill out a form, write a cheque or wander off to the post box. All the customer needs to do is pick up the phone, dial a number (usually a freephone number), place the order and pay by quoting a credit card number.

You don't even need to leave your armchair – let alone your house.

And now, you don't need to read either because there are countless shopping channels on television, so all you need is the TV remote control in one hand and the phone in the other. Armchair shopping is hugely popular but has one significant drawback – you can't go armchair shopping for a specific item. The items offered for sale are selected by the TV channel and they are offered one at a time in sequence. It's rather like sitting in front of a conveyor belt watching the goods come past and waiting until something appears that might be of use to you. You choose to either buy or not buy, and then wait for the next item to be offered for sale. You can't go TV shopping with a specific list of items.

Most TV shopping channels operate a sort of conveyor belt system.

New technology has brought together all of the best features of the other selling methods and wrapped them up in the hi-tech Internet and newly hatched e-commerce.

Shopping using the Internet opens up a whole new world of armchair shopping which is going to become far more widespread.

Numerous companies around the world have been selling via the Internet for years. Some have branched out and now offer online shopping as an alternative to their conventional retail outlets, whilst some companies have set themselves up as online only retailers. These companies don't have shops, just huge warehouses to dispatch orders.

The idea is simple. Previously, if you wanted a book, you'd go to a bookshop. Now, if you want a book, you go online to a virtual bookshop and order it from there. In the real bookshop you would pay by cash, cheque or credit card, in the virtual bookshop you can't use cash, but you can pay by credit or debit card.

Unlike television shopping, Internet shopping allows you to go to the place which sells the items you want to buy.

The weekly groceries

I can spend any amount of time browsing in music shops, computer shops and car showrooms, but top of my list of undesirable activities is food shopping. Followed closely by clothes shopping.

As with all online shopping, you don't have to be physically present in the shop to do your shopping. This means you can shop at any hour of the day or night.

If, like me, you don't enjoy trundling round a supermarket with a shopping trolley that refuses to go where you want it to, being pushed and trodden on by scores of other shoppers who are also fighting to keep their trolley in order, Internet shopping may be for you.

There are now hundreds of retailers worldwide who offer a delivery service to shoppers who, rather than visiting a store in person, choose their goods over the Internet.

Whatever is available at a Tesco store, for example, can also be purchased over the Internet and will be delivered for a small fee. Tesco introduced online shopping in 1997 and provided customers who held a Tesco loyalty card with a free CD ROM which was used to set up their computer with a sort of inventory of items.

Most stores, including Tesco, no longer require a loyalty card.

Today, you can even order the CD online and register by visiting *http://www.tesco.co.uk/* and clicking on 'Check to see if we deliver in your area'.

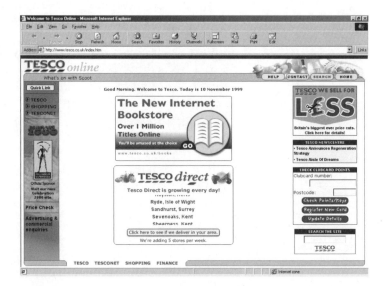

If there is a delivery service, you can register immediately by entering your name and your Club Card number (if you have one). As by this stage you will have entered your postcode, the computer at Tesco will know which road you live in and will offer you all the possible houses in your road, from which you pick your house.

Keep your customer ID safe – you'll need it each time you shop.

You will also need to choose a password which you will have to enter twice. The system will generate a customer ID number.

Once you have successfully registered you can order a CD ROM which contains all the software you need to get you started. You can download the software from the Internet, but the CD ROM is much quicker.

Many supermarkets offer a similar service and more and more are coming online – a trend which is likely to continue.

To find out more about Tesco's Home Shopping, begin by going to *http://www.tesco.co.uk/* and clicking on the Internet Superstore link.

If you're prone to 'impulse' buying, this is a great way to cut down your food bill.

Once you've registered, you must sign-on each time you wish to shop and this involves entering your customer ID and your password.

All the usual benefits – such as discounts that you would get by attending the shop in person, (loyalty card points, 'three-for-two' etc.) – are passed on to you as an Internet shopper.

At present, just about all Internet shops provide you with a sort of menu system through which you must 'track-down' each item you wish to buy.

Description	Item Price	Unit Size	Quantity		
Del Monte Orange Juice 3 X 1 Litre	£2.75	Each	-		+
Del Monte Orange Juice With Bits 1 Litre	£0.99	Each	-		+
Del Monte Pure Orange Juice 1 Litre	£0.95	Each	-		+
Tesco Florida Pure Orange Juice 1litre	£0.75	Each	-		+
Tesco Organic Orange Juice 1 Litre	£0.99	Each	-		+
Tesco Premium Florida Orange Juice & Bits 1 Ltr	£0.89	Each	-		+
Tesco Pure Orange Juice Smooth 1 Litre	£0.69	Each	-		+
Tesco Pure Orange Juice Smooth 4x1 Litre	£2.55	Each	-		+
Tesco Pure Orange Juice Smooth 6x1 Litre	£3.59	Each	-		+
Tesco Pure Orange Juice With Bits 1ltr Carton	£0.69	Each	-		+
Tesco Value Orange Juice 1 Litre Carton	£0.39	Each	-		+

You won't be able to see the items, only their description.

To get to this menu displaying the current selection of fruit juices, you have to wade through several previous menus.

Offline Shopping

Even better than shopping online, is shopping offline. The subtle difference is that you're not running up a phone bill all the time you're selecting your goods. You put together a shopping list offline, then go online to place the order.

Create a file of items you use every week and begin your shopping list with these.

Delivery

The problem with services of this type is that it soon becomes very popular and you'll often need to book the delivery several days in advance. Therefore if you use such a service, it can mean that you'll need to plan the week's meals quite early on during the previous week to ensure you get a delivery time to suit you.

Buying software

One of the major growth areas of Internet selling is computer software. It makes a great deal of sense for both the seller and purchaser to buy over the Internet.

From the seller's point of view, there are fewer overheads. Programs are now so large that they have to be distributed either on a pile of floppy discs or CD ROM – which is now the cheaper of the two options, providing you have enough sales to warrant the cost of producing them.

Selling software over the Internet eliminates the need to hold any stock whatsoever. When someone buys a program, they merely make a copy of the file and pull it across the Internet. It means that transportation costs are now nil.

Compressed, self-extracting files can be moved very quickly over the Net.

From the buyer's point of view, you're not paying for huge quantities of fancy packaging which goes straight in the bin. That, of course, significantly reduces the cost. Quite complex programs can be packaged into a single file, which, when the end-user runs it, will self-unpack and decompress. This feature, together with faster and faster Internet access times, means that software can be downloaded very quickly.

Furthermore, the buyer doesn't need to physically go anywhere to buy the software. It can all be done from the purchaser's home.

This effectively means the end of the printed manual. What happens now is that, wrapped up in the downloaded software package, is the manual as either a text file or a HTML file (which can be viewed with a browser). Sometimes both. The end result is that the user has to either:

* juggle the new software on screen with the software manual,

* print out the manual at his or her own expense, or

* buy the relevant 'in easy steps' book

1 You'll almost always be asked to enter your email address. Some companies will also ask you to enter a password so that you can easily enter the site again.

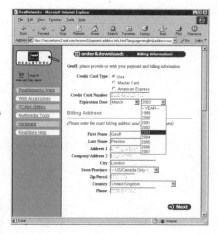

2 You'll need to enter your credit card details and also your full address – for verification purposes.

When you've completed the appropriate sections, the company will check your details (including checking that the credit card is valid). You'll then have an invoice displayed showing what you purchased, the date and price etc.

When that is done, you'll be able to go to the download page to download your purchase.

Good companies such as this one will follow up your order with an email which will again include full details of your purchase.

Going, going, gone...

... to the lady wearing the grey coat and scratching her left ear.

Auctions can be great fun, so I'm told, but if you're frightened of finding that you've bought something because you sneezed at the wrong time, or you scratched your ear just before the gavel fell, why not try an Internet Auction?

The way it works is very clever. Once you've chosen something you want to bid for, you place a maximum bid with the auction house. Nobody else knows what you will be prepared to bid up to as the information is fed into a computer. When all the maximum bids are in, the computer effectively opens the bidding, takes bids, disregards people who have reached their limit and finally finishes up with a buyer.

There's no danger of over-bidding here.

The buyer will have purchased the item by outbidding the other bidders, but will not have gone beyond his predetermined limit – one of the inherent dangers when bidding in a 'real' auction.

To try your hand at an online auction, go to *http://www.amazon.com/*

Airline booking

Booking a flight used to be a painfully long-winded process which always seemed to require a great deal more paperwork than seemed necessary. Certainly, given the choice, I'd rather book a train journey than a plane journey (apart from the destination).

EasyJet proudly boasts that theirs is a ticketless booking system which you can book yourself over the Internet without having to go and sit in a stuffy travel agent's shop.

This is by far the easiest way to book an airline ticket.

Once the booking form has been opened, you are led step by step through a series of screens into which you insert flight times and destination and departure locations. Finally you are asked to enter your credit card details for payment.

EasyJet will confirm your booking by email.

EasyJet's booking system couldn't be easier, especially with the interactive calendar that helps you choose your flight times. Opening the calendar displays the current day and the month. Choose a date and click on one of the Set buttons and the date is automatically entered into the correct place on the booking form.

Finance – Internet banking

Several Banks and Building Societies offer their customers banking via the Internet. The advantage is that you can make transactions, order statements and carry out a variety of other banking tasks from the comfort of your home and at any time of the day or night, 365 days a year. The only thing you can't do is actually withdraw cash – you still need to go to a 'real' bank for that.

First Direct is a branch of HSBC which began offering a very successful 24 hour telephone banking service where customers simply dial a local telephone number and get balances, move money, arrange loans and generally do most things they would do in a traditional bank.

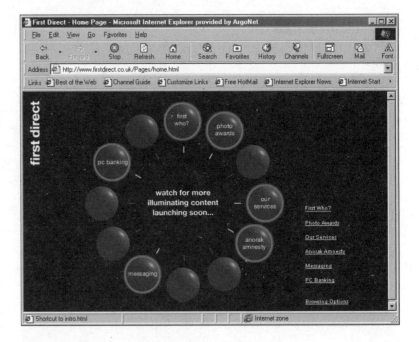

First Direct followed this success by introducing Internet banking to run alongside the telephone service and this too has become very popular. Once enrolled, you will be provided with a CD ROM containing all the software required which is installed on your PC. When the software has been installed and you've registered, you'll have access to your bank account.

Keep your password safe – it's the key to opening your bank account.

The First Direct website can be viewed at *http://www. firstdirect.co.uk/*

There is a link from their homepage which will provide you with information about opening a First Direct bank account.

Internet banking has had some bad press, unfairly in my opinion. Stories abound about hackers intercepting individuals' bank accounts and moving money, but these stories are largely bogus. Internet banking sites like First Direct are as safe as any traditional banking method. Some would argue that they are safer.

Finance – mortgage

This is another relatively new service which looks set to become very popular. Most people who own a home have a mortgage. The question everyone is asking is "Am I paying too much?" A visit to *http://www.emfinance.com/* could provide you with the answer. Within seconds.

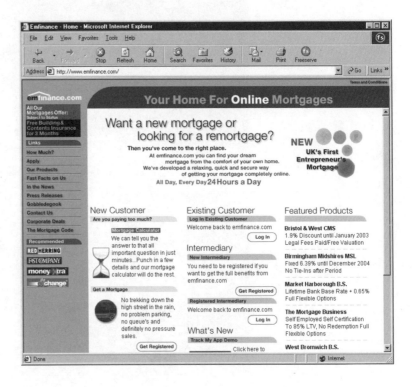

To get the full benefit of this service, register first.

From the homepage, there are links to help you calculate what you should be paying for your mortgage. You'll be required to enter some basic details about your home and the length of mortgage remaining and within a very short space of time, a response will come back telling you if it's worth changing your mortgage lender.

Every variation of mortgage is considered and all from the comfort of your own home.

This type of service is likely to become more widespread over the next few years.

Ordering a credit card

As if to endorse the security of the Internet, one major finance company is offering a credit card which can only be ordered over the Internet.

Egg launched their plastic card at the end of 1999 and offers users a 2% discount in interest on purchases made on the Internet.

If you intend doing a lot of shopping on the Internet, this could be the best credit card to hold.

When you log onto *http://www.egg.com/* you can visit the card-ordering page and complete all of your application details online.

You will then be given an immediate response as to your recommended credit limit. If you agree, the card will be sent, usually within 7 to 10 working days.

Using your card

Internet shopping can only work if you have a credit card, or some sort of arrangement whereby vendors can be paid electronically. But people are reluctant to give away their credit card details to a machine that will transmit its details halfway round the world.

And can you blame them? Contrary to what some might have you believe, the Internet is not a bombproof fortress. There have been numerous examples of fraud carried out on the Internet, and as quickly as one hole is plugged, another seems to gape open.

But let's get it into perspective. Users of credit cards are notoriously lax in their everyday 'conventional' (i.e. non-Internet) business.

Your credit card company will insure you against loss for most high-value transactions.

When we buy goods at a shop counter and pay with a credit card, frequently the salesperson doesn't even bother to check that the signatures on the card and on the receipt are the same. We can all cite examples when we could have signed the slip 'Donald Duck' and nobody would have noticed. And what do we do with the receipt which contains, amongst other things, our credit card number and expiry date? Walk out of the shop and chuck it on the floor. Wander around any supermarket car park and you're sure to find someone's credit card details on a discarded till receipt. Make sure they're not yours.

We have a meal in a restaurant and pay with a credit card. The waiter takes your card and disappears into a dark corner with it for several minutes. What's he doing? Probably what he should be doing, but you wouldn't be the first to have your credit card details copied by a 'here-today-gone-tomorrow' waiter to provide someone with the data to forge your card or use the number to buy goods over the phone or Internet.

Credit card forgery is a huge problem in everyday life. Probably the safest place to use your plastic is on the Net, providing you take sensible precautions.

Precautions

The following precautions should keep you safe...

1. Do not buy from anyone other than a reputable outlet. Giving away your credit card details to a backstreet outfit run by a couple of characters of dubious background is asking for trouble. If what you want to buy is legitimate, buy it from a legitimate outlet.

2. Avoid buying from overseas companies. It's not that they're dishonest, it's just that if something does go wrong it's that much harder to sort it out if the other party is on the other side of the world and doesn't even speak the same language.

3. Only give your credit card details over a secure connection. There is a small chance of someone intercepting your card details over a non-secure connection, but a secure connection is far safer. You'll know when you switch from a secure to a non-secure connection (and vice versa) because a message will appear on the screen.

 Also look out for the padlock symbol at the bottom of your browser, and https instead of http in the Web address.

 You do have the option of preventing the warning appearing when you change between secure and insecure connections. This is not to be recommended.

4. Never send credit card details via email. Email is not a secure service and is easily intercepted. If the company you wish to purchase from is worthwhile purchasing from, they will have a secure service. If they haven't, buy elsewhere. Even sending part of the number with one mailing and the rest with another mailing is not wise.

What will the future bring?

In this business, crystal ball gazing is not to be recommended. Not only is the technology moving very rapidly, it also changes direction very rapidly. A concept which may be on the horizon today may never come to fruition because something else has rendered it obsolete whilst still unborn.

Ordering the weekly food on the Internet can save a considerable amount of time, but it is not always easy to find what you're looking for and then the time you would have spent going to the shop is spent instead sitting in front of a computer. When I visit my local supermarket personally, I always pick up a couple of cartons of fresh juice. I always buy the same and I recognise it from the size of the container, its weight (by 'feel' rather than a known quantity) and colour. I have a vague notion of what it might cost, but that's about it. Trying to pick that particular product online from a written list of 20 other similar products was so difficult that I resorted to raiding the dustbin to retrieve the old carton so that I could copy the description.

Read the chapter on Interaction.

The major development will be in the quality of software which we will use to shop. Picking products from a list is not satisfactory, but virtual reality 3D shopping is already available and just around the corner. Once online, you push your virtual shopping trolley up and down virtual aisles and pick products from virtual shelves. It's much easier, far more friendly and when that technology becomes widespread, then e-commerce will really take off.

But to download that type of software so that it will run at a sensible speed needs faster lines of communication. In other words, you're not going to get real-time virtual reality down a conventional telephone line.

The day is fast approaching when we will all need digital phone lines.

See me, hear me

It's possible to send more than just plain text over the Internet. This chapter shows how you can send voice messages, and both still and moving pictures.

Covers

Chapter Nine

What do you need?

Transmitting sound and graphics (both still and moving) is not as difficult as you might think and doesn't require a great deal of expensive equipment.

In addition to the usual multimedia kit, you'll need a method of inputting sound and a method of capturing video.

Sound

Sound is easy to organise and is very cheap. All you need is a microphone which connects into your sound card. Most

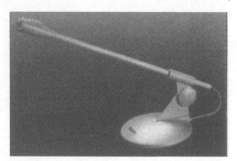

sound cards have an input port which is in the form of a 3.5mm stereo jack socket which the microphone should be plugged into. The microphone then either sits on your desk or attaches to the side of your monitor.

Video

This is a little trickier and slightly more expensive, although not as much as one might think. There are professional video conferencing kits on the market which cost about the same as a top quality desktop PC, but for home use that shouldn't be necessary.

If your computer has a USB port, try and get a video camera which plugs into it, rather than using the parallel port.

You can get excellent results from one of the small web cameras which sit on top of your monitor.

There are at least a dozen to choose from. They're all roughly the same price and have roughly the same features.

The quality, whilst not up to top video conferencing quality, is excellent and belies its low price.

The kits are provided with software which must be installed, but setup is usually then quite straightforward.

For laptop computers, there are small cameras which connect into the PCMCIA socket.

If you have a video camcorder then you may be able to use this as an alternative. If you choose this route, you'll need a video capture card (which will plug into your computer) into which you'll need to connect the camcorder. This solution may give slightly better results, but will not be any cheaper as the cost of a good video capture card is about the same price as a web cam kit which includes all the software needed to set it up and run it.

Some webcams also include the software required to operate a video phone. Generally the results are at least as good as, and frequently better than, 'real' video phones.

Of course to really get the full benefit of this technology you need at least one friend who has similar kit. If you can organise this, you'll find that experimenting with video conferencing, even on a budget, is an exciting and rewarding area of the Internet.

Voice email

The rise in modem speeds has meant that you can now send much larger files across the Internet. One of the more recent developments has been Voice email.

There are several programs capable of recording and then sending the recordings, but the easiest is Voice EMail by Bonzi.

The program is available free from Bonzi's website at *http://www.bonzi.com/* as a limited use evaluation version. If you like it, you can purchase and download the full version.

When the program has been installed and run, a small toolbar will be displayed in the top right corner of the screen. To create a message, click on the Create button.

This opens the window in which you can create your voice email.

If you have a digital camera or webcam you can include a picture and that will be sent as well.

Creating the message is a simple matter of entering the email address of the recipient and speaking into the microphone to record your message.

Receiving voice email

The recipient collects their email in the usual way, with the normal email program (probably Outlook Express or Netscape Messenger). Among the new messages will be the following...

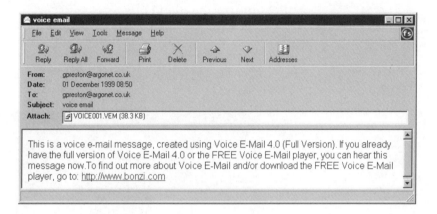

The voice message will be included as an attachment. The text message is automatically generated to tell the recipient the s/he will need Voice EMail to read it.

When the recipient has installed Voice Email (either the evaluation version or the full version) they will be able hear your message and, if you included a picture, see who sent it.

The recipient doesn't need to buy the program to hear your message as there is a free reader on Bonzi's website.

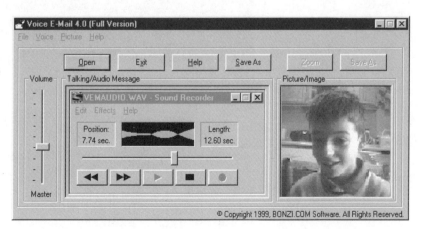

Video email

The next best thing to sending a voice email is to send a video mail. Logitech's web camera comes with a very versatile program that allows you to record a short film and email it.

Sending a video mail

All of the video email programs are slightly different, but most require just three steps...

| Click on the Video icon and begin recording your video.

Video uses up lots of memory. You won't be able to email a feature length film.

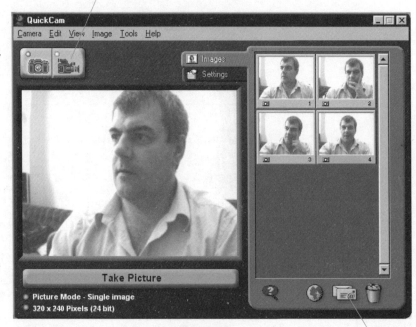

Place the camera so that you can look straight into it. That way, the recipient will think you're talking to them.

2 When you've completed it you can review it, and when you're happy with it, click the Email icon.

3 You'll then be asked to enter the email address of the recipient.

As soon as you're ready to send it, the program will connect you to the Internet and send it.

Receiving a video mail

When the recipient next downloads his email, there will be a message generated by the computer, with your movie file attached. Outlook Express displays a paper clip in the top right of the message, and clicking on it will give the recipient the opportunity of either playing it or saving it.

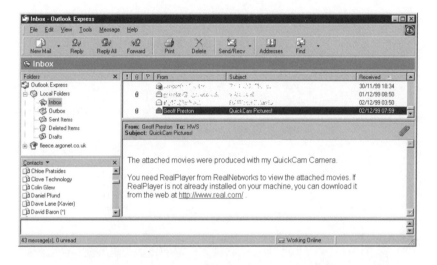

It's worth downloading Real Player even if you don't anticipate playing video mails.

To play the message the recipient must have Real Player which is a free download from *http://www.real.com/*

Live video

We started with sending text, then sending recorded voice. The next stage was to send recorded video. The ultimate is to send and receive live video simultaneously. This is full video conferencing.

Hardware

To do any serious video conferencing you need some fairly expensive kit, which is purpose-designed to enable you to have a meeting with several others who could be on opposite sides of the world.

If you have a camera and a microphone, you probably will have everything you need to operate a modest conference. In fact, you can manage without the camera – but that will mean that the other person will not be able to see you.

Software

If you have Internet Explorer 5, then you have Microsoft NetMeeting and this will be adequate for most people's needs at home.

This demonstration was set up on opposite sides of the same room, but the computers could have been on opposite sides of the world.

NetMeeting is quite straightforward to set up and comes with excellent on-screen help to guide you through the setup procedure.

With NetMeeting, you can see and hear the person you are talking to, and they can see and hear you, but live. The video frames are a little jumpy but considering how much data is being transmitted and received, it's pretty good. Apart from this slight imperfection, it's just like having a conversation with a person face to face.

This program also features an interactive whiteboard which both parties can share.

Even very young children can use this technology.

This technology will become more widespread during the next few years, particularly in education where children will be able to hold conversations with other children in this country and overseas. And all for the cost of a local telephone call.

Web cams

Even if you don't have a web camera, you can still enjoy them. Around the world are placed hundreds of cameras which are connected to the Internet and completely unmanned.

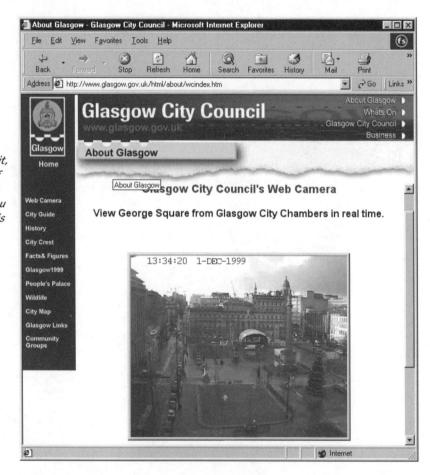

If you're planning a visit, check to see if there's a local webcam so you can see what the weather is doing.

A visit to *http://www.liveviews.org/* will provide a list of many of the webcams throughout the world. What they display is not a moving picture, nor just a still picture. What you get is time-lapse photography with the frames being updated every 15-30 seconds or thereabouts.

Visiting this site will also provide information about how you could set up your own webcam.

Music on the Web

This chapter shows you how to get music from the Internet, how to use it and how to use the Internet to catalogue your CD collection.

Covers

Chapter Ten

Introduction

If you like to listen to music by a particular group, singer or composer, the chances are you'll go to your local music shop and buy a plastic disc containing recordings of your chosen music. It will come in a special protective case, probably with pictures and information about the artist. The shop will carefully wrap your purchase and you'll pay for it before trundling back home to insert it into a special player.

The only variation with this activity in recent years has been the change from black discs (vinyl records) to silver discs (Compact discs).

Since the advent of affordable record players, this is how we have collected and played our favourite music. But getting music you like doesn't have to be like this, and if some people have their way, it won't be for much longer.

Although theoretically not as good as CDs, in reality few people can tell the difference.

The current trend is towards music files called MP3. These are computer files of digital recordings which can be downloaded from the Internet and played on your computer. Previously, digital recordings stored as computer files used copious quantities of disc space and clearly were not really suitable for downloading from the Internet. The average track on a Compact Disc is about 35Mb.

Personally I can't tell the difference between a CD on my hi-fi and MP3 on my computer.

MP3 recordings are much smaller but as far as the average person is concerned, no less perfect. This is because they have been created with all the sounds that humans can't hear removed. This reduces them to about one-tenth of their original size which works out at just over 1Mb per minute of music. The average song track is about 3 minutes which translates to about 3-3.5Mb which doesn't take too long to download, but the quality is still excellent.

To get the full value of digital sound on your computer you'll need a good sound card and very good speakers. Most multimedia computers are sold with only a passable sound card, and speakers that often aren't up to even that standard. But these will be good enough to get you going.

Ideally you need a 32bit sound card and good quality mains powered and amplified stereo speakers, preferably with a sub-woofer to really bring the sound alive. Anything less will produce sound which is less pure, but still very acceptable.

If you're going to get seriously involved with MP3, buy a good sound card and speakers.

To download the MP3 files, you really do need a fast modem otherwise is will take a long time.

You'll also need a credit card because many of the songs are chargeable. Many are free, but it seems that all the songs that have ever been heard of, by artists that are anything more than vaguely familiar, require to be paid for, although the cost can work out much less than you think.

Where do I get MP3 files?

There are several sites from which you can download files, but one of the most popular is MP3 Central which is at *http://music.lycos.com/mp3/*

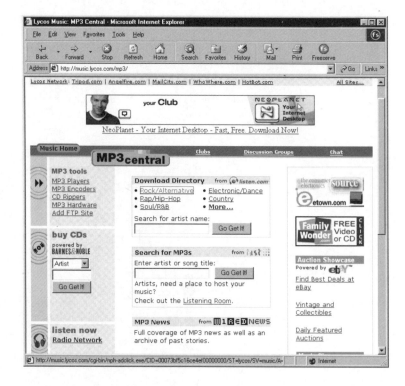

Refer to the chapter on Downloading for more details about capturing MP3 files.

MP3 is the most widely searched for word – even more than sex.

At MP3 Central you can search for MP3 recordings by either song name or artist name. The library is huge and is getting larger by the hour.

It's also worth investigating *http://mp3.box.sk/* which has a list of all the best MP3 search engines.

Do not get involved with illegal files; pay for legitimate ones.

Other legitimate MP3 sites exist, but so do several less legitimate ones. Some sites contain huge quantities of pirated music which is either being sold off cheap or given away.

These should be avoided at all costs, as should individuals who attach MP3 files to news postings or to emails.

Although not strictly an Internet item, this is a useful accessory for MP3 fans.

Another way of getting MP3 files is to copy them from your own music CDs using CD ripper software.

Many of the MP3 sites include CD ripper software or provide links to other sites which have it. These are programs that will read a recording on a music CD and convert it into an MP3 file. There are lots available either free or for a small fee.

You simply place your music CD into your CD ROM drive in your PC and run the software. You choose a track to rip and the program creates an MP3 file from it (usually faster than real time).

Be aware of the laws on copyright.

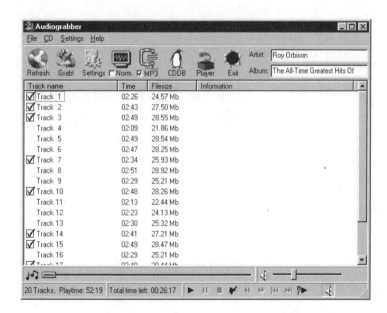

Audiograbber is one of the best and is available from TUCOWS' website at *http://www.tucows.com/*

Note

Copying recordings is illegal. Strictly, it's illegal to copy tracks from Compact Discs onto cassette tape, Mini Disc or MP3 files for you own use. It's really a very serious offence to convert tracks from Compact Discs into MP3 format and distribute them over the Internet.

What do I need to play MP3?

All you need to play MP3 files on your computer is a software MP3 player, of which there are several and mostly free.

Top of the list must be Sonique which is distributed free by Lycos and can be found at *http://music.lycos.com/*

Sonique can be displayed in three different sizes, but only the largest version gives access to all of the features.

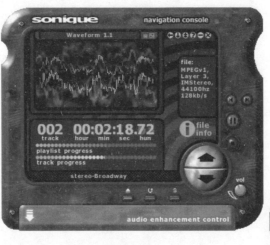

Sonique can also play Web radio.

Sonique has several displays including information about the current track and a graphical output of the music being played.

Looking as though it were carved from a solid piece of granite, Sonique does not run in the usual and familiar Microsoft window, but it does behave in much the same way as a window (you can move it around, place it behind other windows etc.).

The controls allow you to play any number of tracks and there is scope for repeating tracks as well as skipping.

The audio enhancement panel provides scope for setting the balance and the speed and pitch of the playback.

MP3 files that have previously been downloaded and saved onto your computer can be dragged from filer windows into Sonique and played through your computer's sound system.

Although you can use previously downloaded MP3 files with Sonique, this program will log onto the Internet and search for particular files if you wish. This is generally a better way of downloading and importing files as Sonique can do it all in one operation.

Sonique can connect to the Internet and download MP3 files for you.

Once you have amassed your collection of MP3 files you can 'tell' Sonique where they are and they will be played whenever you run Sonique. The songs can be changed around just as you would do with CDs or Mini Discs.

If Sonique is too gimmicky, then try Xing's MP3 player which is also free as part of their CD ripper software, AudioCatalyst.

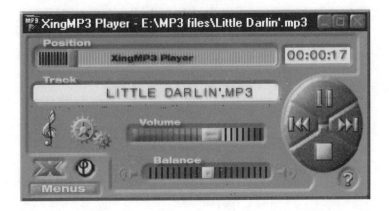

Xing's MP3 player is much more straightforward, although it doesn't have all of the features of Sonique.

The limited use, but free, AudioCatalyst, together with Xing's MP3 player, can be obtained from Xing's website at *http://www.xingtech.com/*

If you like the CD ripper, there's a small charge for the fully working version.

MP3 on the move

Although not strictly about the Internet, this is a handy accessory for users of MP3 files downloaded from the Internet.

The advantage of cassettes, Mini Discs and CDs is that they can be played on portable equipment and carried around with you. Portable players have been around for several years but they all suffer from one drawback – the moving parts frequently don't like being moved. Cassette players chew up the cassette tapes and CD players tend to jump and skip if they're knocked or jogged. Mini Disc players looked to be about the best solution, until the arrival of portable MP3 players.

With a portable MP3 player you can copy your MP3 files from your PC and carry them around with you.

Portable MP3 players

The first thing you'll notice is that they are incredibly light and this is largely due to the fact that they don't contain a heavy electric motor to turn a disc or spool a tape. In fact, they have no moving parts, other than a couple of touch buttons to control it.

For this reason, many don't even have the facility of connecting to an external (mains) power supply.

As the batteries don't have to drive a heavy electric motor, these players run for a long time on (usually) a single 1.5 volt battery.

There are several models available and all are currently in the same approximate price range as portable mini disc players. Most connect to your PC via the parallel (printer) port, although some use the serial port and fewer use the USB (Universal Serial Bus). Of them all, the USB models seem to be the most convenient, providing you've got a USB port on your computer.

Most have 32 Mb of storage which is about 10-12 tracks (depending on the length of the tracks), but they can also house special memory cards (called Compact Flash) which will usually add a further 32Mb.

Cook your own CDs

Slightly less ultra-hi-tech than MP3 files, but nevertheless well worth considering, is the growing number of websites which offer you the chance to create your own CD from a list of songs.

This is a great way to buy compilation CDs.

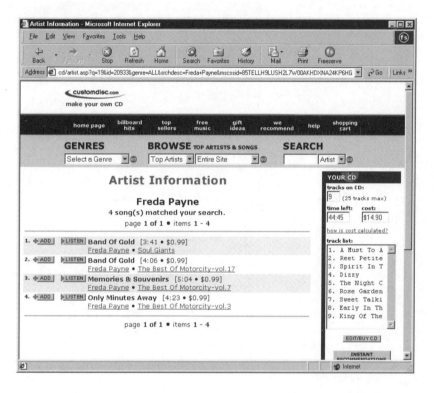

This method of buying CDs is likely to become very popular.

There are several sites which offer this service e.g. Customdisc at *http://www.customdisc.com/* and Razorcuts at *http://www.razorcuts.co.uk/*

When you log onto one of the sites, you can search through its database for the songs that are available. You can preview any of the songs and if you like them, add them to your 'shopping trolley'. You can normally collect up to 25 tracks or a little over an hour's worth of music. There is a cost per track plus a basic price for the service.

When you've completed your disc and paid for it via credit card, the company produces the CD and posts it to you.

Web radio

Music while you work takes on a whole new meaning with radio coming through the Internet whilst you are using your computer.

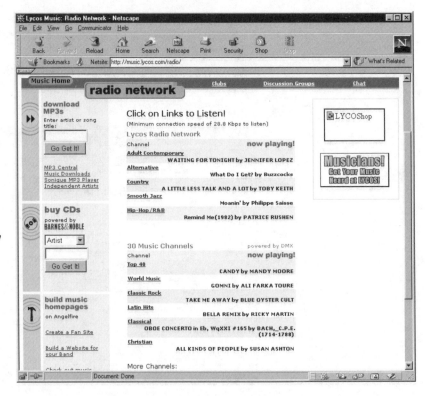

You can also play radio with Sonique.

A visit to *http://music.lycos.com/radio/* takes you to one of the several websites that transmit radio broadcasts via the Internet.

You can choose from a wide range of channels (in Lycos' case there are over 30) and you're even told what is playing at a particular moment on each of the channels.

You choose the station by clicking on its name and (in the case of Lycos) you will be taken to a setup page where you will need to specify a few important points about the system you're running.

It's important to correctly configure the options to get the radio working properly. You must first choose the type of connection you have – either a dial-up account or ISDN connection. If you have ISDN then you can choose to show a video of the music at the same time it's playing.

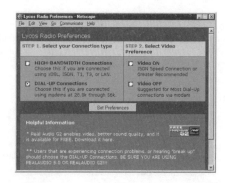

If you only have a dial-up connection, it's probably best to elect not to show the video as it will take too long to download. The result could be that the sound becomes intermingled with periods of silence and your computer could slow down to the point where you'd be forgiven for thinking it had stopped altogether.

Although the video looks great, it ties up your computer for longer periods.

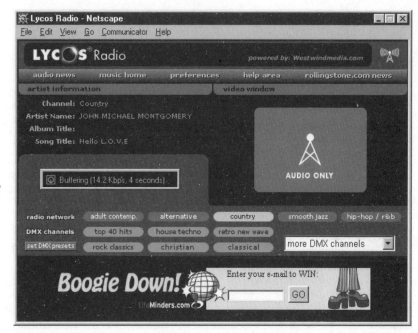

Once you're in, you can change channels with exactly the same freedom as you can with a conventional radio.

Catalogue your CD collection

It's long been known that music Compact Discs can be played on your computer's CD drive. To help with this pursuit there have been countless virtual CD players to enable you to control the tracks and the discs – if you have more than one CD drive.

It then came about that the name of the CD and the track titles could be displayed whilst the music was playing by matching a CD's serial number to a database which the user had to build himself or herself.

Some recordings marketed in certain countries can get confused with similar recordings intended for other countries.

Typing in all of the track titles for even a modest CD collection is a time consuming task. Not to mention tedious.

The Deluxe CD player supplied with Windows 98 Plus is not, as many thought, yet another version of the same thing. This player has one fundamental difference. When you insert a music CD that you haven't used before, the program will connect itself to the Internet and access a website that holds a catalogue of music CDs.

This is an excellent way to catalogue your CD collection.

The serial number of the CD will be matched against the database held on the website and, if a match is made, it will download the title of the CD together with the names of the tracks.

In addition to pulling down the CD details, it will, if you choose, connect you to a website that will give you more information about the artist featured on the current CD.

Alternatively, *http://www.cddb.com/* will supply the full details of the music CD in your drive which can be copied as a text file.

Downloading

There are countless programs on the Internet which can be downloaded and run on your computer. But this chapter is about more than getting free programs. It also covers grabbing text and graphics from the Web.

Covers

Chapter Eleven

Downloading drivers

When you buy a new piece of hardware for your PC (e.g. printers, scanners, modems, sound cards), it will come with driver software. In simple terms, the software 'tells' the computer what the product is, what settings are available and how the computer is to communicate with the hardware.

Always use the latest drivers.

Although the hardware itself doesn't change (until the manufacturer brings out a new model) the software drivers are regularly updated and improved upon. It is usually in the user's best interests to run the latest drivers for their computer hardware and the best place to get the latest driver is from the manufacturer's website.

All of the top manufacturers have websites on which they store the latest versions of their drivers. In most cases, the upgrades are free.

Some of the main sites containing drivers are...

Brother	—	*http://www.brother.com/*
Epson	—	*http://www.epson.com/*
Canon	—	*http://www.canon.com/*
Hewlett Packard	—	*http://www.hp.com/*
Mustek	—	*http://www.mustek.com/*
D-Link	—	*http://www.dlink.com/*
3Com	—	*http://www.3com.com/*
ATI	—	*http://www.ati.com/*
Fujitsu	—	*http://www.fujitsu.com/*
Microtek	—	*http://www.microtek.com/*
Panasonic	—	*http://www.panasonic.com/*
Quantum	—	*http://www.quantum.com/*
Seagate	—	*http://www.seagate.com/*

When buying a new piece of hardware, always take note of the manufacturer's website.

Once you have arrived at the website, look for the link that goes to the section with the latest drivers. This will often be signposted Software Support. Sometimes, as in the Hewlett Packard site, it is clearly marked.

Different sites are mapped out in different ways, but in most cases you'll have to carry out the same procedures, although not necessarily in the order outlined here. This commentary is based on Hewlett Packard's site which is a model of clarity and good web page design.

Make sure you know the exact make and model of the hardware.

Find the link to the area that has the drivers.

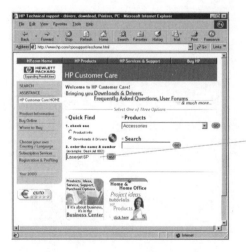

2 You'll need to specify the type of product (printer, scanner etc.) and the model number.

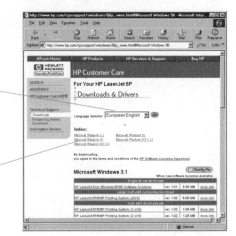

3 At some point you'll be asked to specify the language for the driver....

4 ...and the operating system you are using.

Even though this software is provided free, copyright laws still apply.

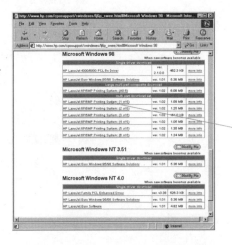

5 Choose a driver by clicking on the link.

Many companies provide their drivers in two forms – either as a single large file or as a number of smaller files, each of which will save onto one high density floppy disc.

If the driver is intended only to be used on the computer which is being used to download it, select the single large file. If you want to use it on another computer, choose the multiple smaller files and transfer them onto floppy discs when you've downloaded them.

6 A dialog will open offering the choice of either saving the program or running it. Choose Save... then click OK...

Downloads usually come as compressed self-extracting files. Double-clicking them will decompress them and begin installation.

7 ...and a dialog will open giving you the chance to choose a location. The filename determined by the manufacturer will be visible in the Name: window. Change this to something more meaningful if you wish then click Save.

8 The file will now download and the window will show you the current status.

When it's finished downloading, go to the file and double-click on it. It will then unpack itself and begin installing.

Saving Web pages

Everything that can be viewed on a Web page can be captured either for future reference or to be included in a document of your own.

This means that including pictures and diagrams in your documents no longer requires that you buy expensive products like a digital camera or scanner.

If you see something that you wish to quote, the text can easily be copied into your document.

If you do use this feature, always quote the source of the material in your work. It's not reasonable to pinch someone's efforts and pass them off as your own.

Web pages in their entirety can be saved, but frequently the page doesn't re-display exactly the same. This is because the pictures are often not included.

| Go to File at the top left of the screen.

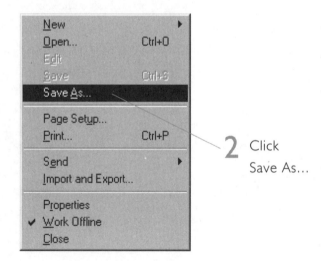

2 Click
Save As...

If you want to learn how Web pages are written, you could view the source.

Saving pictures

Any picture or icon displayed on a Web page can be saved and, in most cases, used in another document.

| With the mouse pointer over a picture you wish to save, click the right mouse button to display a menu.

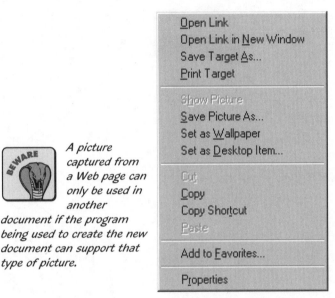

(Internet Explorer)

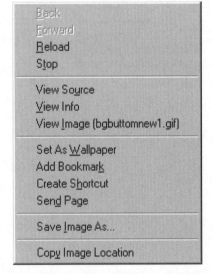

(Netscape Navigator)

A picture captured from a Web page can only be used in another document if the program being used to create the new document can support that type of picture.

2 From the menu, select Save Image As... or Save Picture As....

3 A standard Save dialog will be displayed in which you can choose the name and destination of the file. Clicking on the Save button will save the picture.

Capturing text

The easiest way to capture text is to use the copy and paste facility.

This works in exactly the same way with both browsers. Text can be pasted into virtually every program that supports text.

1 Mark the section of text on the Web page that you wish to use by dragging the mouse pointer over the text whilst holding down the left mouse button.

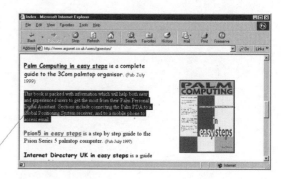

2 Press Ctrl+C to copy the text into an area of the computer's memory called the Clipboard.

3 Open the document you wish to put the copied text into and, with the cursor in the place you wish to place the text, click the left mouse button.

Sometimes Web designers force a new line by using a Return. This can have strange effects when the text goes into another document. Use delete to remove unwanted Returns.

4 Paste the text by pressing Ctrl+V

Do-it-yourself

Most ISPs provide webspace for you and your family to use. Many people don't bother, but creating a family website can be a great deal of fun as well as being a valuable skill to learn. This chapter shows you how to get started.

Covers

Chapter Twelve

Your own website

As outlined in the introduction, anyone can join the World Wide Web and many Internet Service Providers not only make it easy, but positively encourage it.

Of the 15 free ISPs used to research this book, all gave at least 5 Mb of Web space free, and some gave as much as 20 Mb. A couple of years ago there was a significant charge for even 5 Mb of Web space. But for most people, this is more than enough to create their personal website.

How it works

The basic principle is that you create your Web pages and test them on your computer. When you are satisfied that they work, you move them to your ISP, from where the rest of the world can access them, as long as they have the address.

Creating a website can be frustrating and time consuming, but a great deal of fun.

As time goes by, you will want (or need) to update pages, and add pages to your website. This is done on your computer, and these too will be sent to your ISP to become part of your website, after thorough testing.

Don't get over ambitious

Take a quick scan around the Internet and you will see a huge number of very well constructed pages. Don't think you'll be able to do something as good as these overnight. Some of the commercial sites are maintained by webmasters and webmistresses who spend their whole life creating Web pages and apparently do little or nothing else. And they've been doing it for a long time.

However, you can produce some very creditable Web pages with relative ease. As you progress you'll be able to incorporate new features into your site.

There are two things which come out of this. First, the standard of a website will be commensurate with the creator's Web building ability. As soon as he or she learns a new trick, it will soon be incorporated into the site.

Secondly, websites are never finished.

What do I need?

You could probably get away with not having to buy anything to create your website. The most important thing you'll need is a program that can generate Web pages. This can be done in three ways.

The hard way

You can normally drag and drop a HTML file into a text document window.

Every computer has some sort of text editor which can be used to create Web pages. This means that everyone should be able to create a Web page.

Web pages are created using a language called HTML – HyperText Markup Language. You can type the contents of a Web page into the text editor and save it as a HTML document instead of a text document.

Try typing in this program and saving it as *Test.html*...

```
<HTML>

<HEAD>

<TITLE> Computer Step </TITLE>

</HEAD>

<BODY>

<MARQUEE> in easy steps books make understanding computers easy

</MARQUEE>

</BODY>

</HTML>
```

'HTML in easy steps' is an excellent introduction to HTML programming.

When you drag and drop *Test.html* into a browser window you should see the title 'Computer Step' on the top left of the window title bar and the words 'in easy steps books make understanding computers easy' scrolling across the screen (assuming your browser supports scrolling text).

An easier way

Many programs will output files as a Web page. Both Microsoft Word and Microsoft Publisher can, but there are several others.

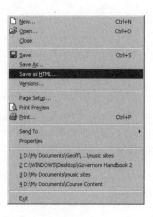

The way to check if a particular program will create Web pages is to open a document, click on File on the menu bar at the top of the screen, and look to see if Save as HTML appears in the menu.

If it does, you can use that program to create Web pages.

Not everything you do in a word processor will translate into a Web page.

Alternatively, from the File menu, click on Save as... and at the very bottom of the save dialog is a panel alongside Save as type:. Click on the panel and a menu of possible filetypes will open. Check to see if HTML is there. If it is, it means that that program can output files in HTML and therefore can be used to generate Web pages.

But a word of caution. In most cases, the program you choose to use to output HTML will almost certainly be capable of doing far more than HTML can handle. The result will be that the document you so carefully laid out may not look exactly the same when translated into HTML. In particular, different sections may not sit alongside each other correctly.

The other problem is that most word processors can handle a variety of graphic objects. If using a word processor to create Web pages, stick to GIF and JPEG graphics only.

The easiest way

By far the easiest way to create Web pages is to use a dedicated Web page designer.

When installing Microsoft's Internet Explorer suite you will have had the option of installing FrontPage Express which is Microsoft's Web page editor.

If you use Netscape Communicator, then you will have Composer as part of the package.

Most of the top websites are created using a variety of tools, including coding raw HTML.

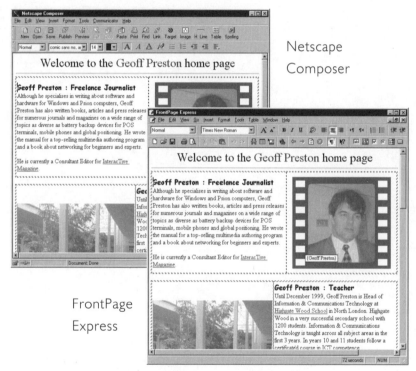

Netscape Composer

FrontPage Express

These programs (and others which can be purchased in addition to these) provide easy access to all of the tools required to make up pages in HTML. They look and operate in much the same way as a document processor such as Word or Publisher, but they won't let you do anything that can't be translated into HTML (a disadvantage of the previous method).

Linking pages

Have a go at creating a couple of simple Web pages and experimenting with some HTML codes.

Even if you intend using a special editor, it's worth doing a little experimenting with HTML so you can get a feel of what it can do and how it works.

If you haven't already done so, create the Web page using a text editor as described on page 187. Save it as *Test.html*.

To make alterations to it, drag the file from the filer window into a text document window.

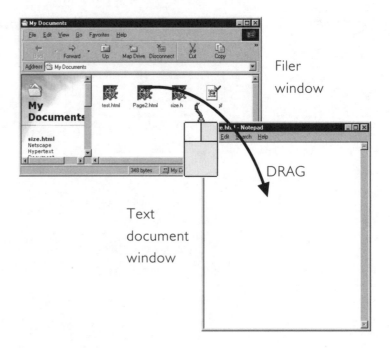

Filer window

Text document window

DRAG

Websites are pages of information which are connected using hyperlinks. This is the part that frightens off most people, but it really isn't difficult to grasp, or to execute.

Having created a simple Web page, drag it into a document window and add the following line immediately before the second from last line...

<A HREF="Page2.html">Click here</A>

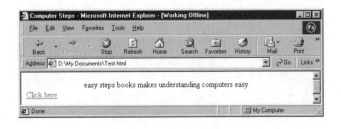

Copy these instructions exactly as they appear here, including the chevrons '<' and '>'.

Next create a new page and enter the following...

\<HTML>

\<HEAD>

\<TITLE> Page Two \</TITLE>

\</HEAD>

\<BODY>

\<P> This should be another page.

\</P>

\<A HREF="Test.html"> Return to 1st page\</A>

\</BODY>

These two pages hardly constitute a website, but this is the basis upon which all websites are created.

\</HTML>

Save this document as *Page2.html*.

Now, when you drop *Test.html* into your browser, you should see an underlined link under the scrolling text. Clicking on this link should open the second document which should contain an underlined link which will return you to the first page.

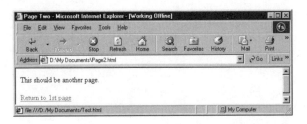

Pretty text

The text used previously will be fine, although it will be all the same colour and all the same size.

Text colour

Text colour is determined by stating the quantities of red, green and blue. These numbers are quoted using a strange numbering system called hexadecimal. Put simply, it uses numbers 0 to 9 and then letters A to F.

Placing ...

You must use COLOR and not COLOUR.

```
<FONT COLOR="#FFFFFF">
```

...will change the following text to white. Whilst...

```
<FONT COLOR="#000000">
```

...will change it to black.

Each pair of digits represents each of the colours red, green and blue in that order so...

```
<FONT COLOR="#FF0000">
```

...will give pure red, whilst...

```
<FONT COLOR="#00FF00">
```

...will give pure green, and...

If each pair of digits is the same, you'll get a shade of grey.

```
<FONT COLOR="#0000FF">
```

...gives pure blue.

You can mix colours and you can use different quantities of each colour so that...

```
<FONT COLOR="#AA0088">
```

...gives a sort of purple, and...

```
<FONT COLOR="#44AACC">
```

...gives a rather fetching shade of sky blue.

Text size

To change the text size, use the command...

`<FONT SIZE=`*n*`>`

...where *n* is a number between 1 and 7.

Use the larger
size for titles
only.

Using the command...

`</FONT>`

...changes the font size back to what it was before it was last changed.

If the person
looking at your
page doesn't
have the font
you specified,
the page may not be
displayed properly.

Font style

You can change the style of the font (the typeface) using...

`<FONT FACE = "`*fontname*`">`

...where *fontname* is the name of the font.

Adding a picture

Sooner or later you will want to add some graphics to your Web pages. The instruction is...

<IMG SRC="*name*.gif">

Initially, the safest way is to keep the document and the picture together.

...where *name*.gif is the filename of a picture, including the three digit DOS suffix. The picture should be placed in the same filer window as the HTML document or it must have its location specified as part of the name.

Other useful commands

The list of HTML commands is long, and it's difficult to choose a small number to give a taste of what can be done. Here are some of the most popular...

<BODY BGCOLOR="#*rrggbb*">	sets the background colour for the whole page.
<HR>	draws a horizontal line across the page
<FONT SIZE=+1>	increases the font size by one
<FONT SIZE=-1>	decreases the font size by one
<P ALIGN="*p*">	aligns text where *p* is either center, left or right
<I>	italicises text
</I>	switches off italics
<B>	emboldens text
</B>	switches off emboldened text

This is but a small selection of the HTML commands available to you.

All commands go between < and >. A slash (/) switches off a previously issued command.

Where to get Web resources

The best place to get resources for your website is, unsurprisingly, on the Web.

The easiest way to track down these resources is to go to Yahoo (*http://www.yahoo.com/*) and enter GIF in the search field.

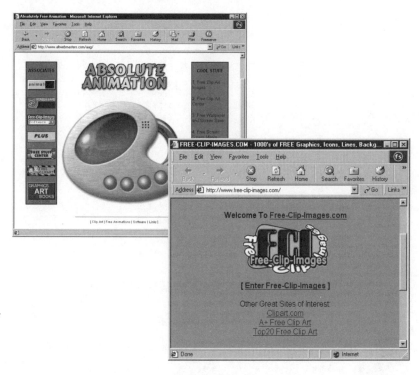

Use the resources that are being freely given away rather than pinching them from someone else's website.

The resulting list provides links to countless sites offering free use of...

animated GIFs — little animations

digitised photos — quality pictures in the correct format

icons — to guide the user around your site.

You should find a great deal of material to enhance your website.

Uploading

Check, check and check again before uploading your website.

When you have completed your Web pages and you have tested them thoroughly to ensure that everything works as it should, it must be sent to your Internet Service Provider. This is called uploading.

Different ISPs have slightly different arrangements for uploading. Some companies provide their own uploader, like Argonet who provide Webload for PCs, and have a version for Macs as well. Webload will look for Web pages that have been altered and, by default, will only attempt to upload those. Pages that have been deleted between the last upload and the current upload will be removed from the website.

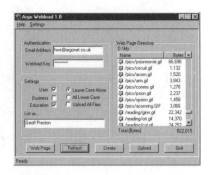

If your ISP does not provide such a program, you'll need to use the uploader which is part of the editor you are using to create your website.

Even the slightest alteration means that the relevant page(s) will need to be uploaded.

If you choose this route, you'll need to check a few things with your ISP before you can upload. You may already have been supplied with the information, but you will usually need to know the name of the first page of your website. (This might be *home.html* or *index.html* or something similar.) The other piece of information you'll need is your URL – the Internet address you'll need to enter to access your website from anywhere in the world.

You may have to choose which pages you want uploaded. The first time it will be all of them, but from then on you will only need to upload pages that have been changed or new pages that have been added.

Advertising your site

Tell your friends about your website first.

For some, just building a modest website is sufficient and they don't feel the need to advertise it, nor do they feel let down if nobody visits it. But it would be a shame not to share all your hard work with others. Perhaps just close friends, perhaps the whole world.

Before you do announce your creation, put a counter on the front page which records how many people have visited your site. Many ISPs supply one, but if your ISP doesn't, go to *http://www.dbasic.com/counter/* and use their counter, which includes instructions.

Test your site carefully before announcing it to the world.

Notifying close friends is easy. Email them, and include in your email signature the address of your website. If they are using a modern email program then they will just need to click on the address to be taken there.

Notifying the rest of the world is no less easy now that sites such as *http://www.submit-it.com/* have come online.

If your site is on a specific theme, why not join a webring?

Once you've entered your details (and paid a small fee) details of your site will be sent to a variety of search engines.

What else do I need?

If you have an Internet account with personal Web space and you have Internet Explorer or Netscape Communicator then you have everything you actually *need*. With this, all you will be able to do is produce a website with lots of text, illustrated with a few bits of clip art you picked up from here and there.

Icons and buttons

Icons and simple buttons which are personal to you can be produced using a paint program, as long as it will output as a GIF file which is the favoured file format for graphics on the Web. There are some programs which will enable you to produce animated icons.

You can spend a small fortune on goodies to enhance your website, but you should not buy them for this purpose alone.

Photos

You will doubtless want to include some pictures, possibly photographs on your website. These can be captured in one of two ways. The more expensive way is to buy a digital camera. Unlike conventional cameras, a digital camera takes pictures and saves them either to disc or to memory within the camera. These pictures can then be transferred to your computer as either a GIF file or a JPEG file. (For pictures, JPEG is generally reckoned to be the better option.)

The cheaper option is to buy a scanner. Flatbed scanners which connect to your computer via either the parallel or (preferably) a USB port are now incredibly cheap. Your old family photographs can then be scanned and dropped into your website. In some respects this is a better buy than the camera as it can be used for so many other things including scanning pages of text and translating them into editable text.

Video

If you have a means of capturing video such as a webcam, you can include small movies on your Web page, but don't go overboard with this feature. They can take a long time to download.

The limitation is your imagination, not your pocket.

Finance on the Web

Money, it is said, makes the world go round. The Internet is a great place to carry out your financial dealings as well as for looking up information about financial deals and getting advice on your finances, both immediate and long term. Make sure that the site from which you pull down information is regularly updated.

Covers

Chapter Thirteen

Clearing banks

Most major banks have websites and it's worth checking them out from time to time to see who has the best deals for loans and deposits. As one would expect from large multinational companies, the sites are very well organised and contain lots of useful information, although one shouldn't forget these sites are also adverts.

Commonwealth Bank of Australia	*http://www.commbank.com.au/*
Trust Bank of N. Zealand	*http://www.trustbank.co.nz/*
Royal Bank of Canada	*http://www.royalbank.com/*
NatWest	*http://www.natwest.com/*

These sites contain some valuable financial information.

More and more banks are offering online banking and in many cases you can sign up through the bank's website.

Credit cards

Two of the world's major credit cards have websites in which they provide a great deal of information about their cards and other services they provide, such as insurance.

 Look out for special offers.

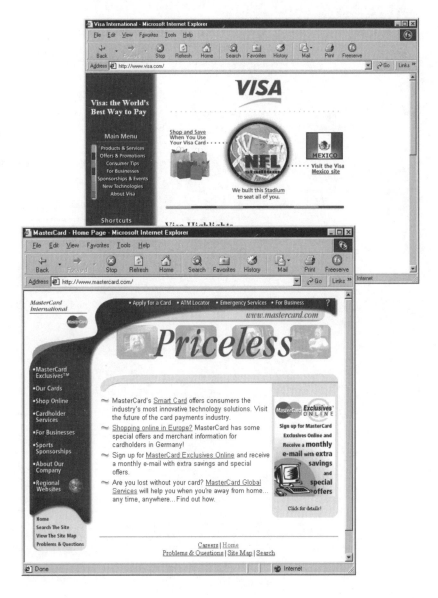

Visa is at *http://www.visa.com/* and MasterCard is at *http://www.mastercard.com/*

Share trading

For those who enjoy dabbling with shares, this site is invaluable. Amongst other features, it lists the FTSI prices which can be displayed either in alphabetical order or by the amount they rose or fell.

Additional information is available about Personal Equity Plans or PEPs, as well as other long term financial investments.

If you do decide to dabble in shares, be warned – a great many people have made a killing, but a great many more have lost virtually everything.

This site has all the latest prices and is very accurate.

Shares can (and do) go down as well as up.

But this is a good site to begin with because it does explain what it's all about and guides you through the process. The Interactive Investor may be found by going to *http://www.iii.co.uk/*

Also check out Wall Street prices which are constantly updated at *http://www.wallstreetcity.com/*

An alternative site for getting the latest prices on your shares is the E★Trade site at *http://www.etrade.com/* and *http://www.etrade.co.uk/*

Information you provide may be passed on to other reputable companies who offer goods and services which may be of interest to you. This can be suppressed if required.

The E★Trade website contains everything you need to make investment decisions. The advantage of a well maintained site such as this is that the prices are always up to date.

To get the most from this site you should register. The online form requires that you provide some security information which you'll need to quote when you re-enter the site.

Once registered, you'll have access to a full range of financial services to enable you to be on a level playing field with the professionals.

E★Trade also provide free real time quotes, with low commission rates.

Interactive Finance Services

If you own your home, you can borrow money against it for all manner of purchases.

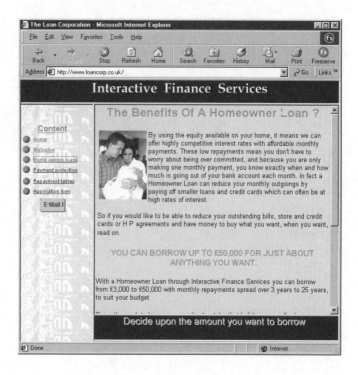

Your home could be at risk if you do not keep up payments on a mortgage or other loan secured on it.

This is called a secured loan because your house is the security – if you can't or won't repay the loan, the lender could take your house from you and sell it to recover the outstanding debt. The advantage of a secured, as opposed to an unsecured, loan is that the interest charges are much, much lower.

This website, like many others springing up around the world, offers loans to homeowners at very competitive rates. You apply for a loan over the Internet by completing an online registration form giving the usual information about salary and expenditure.

The reply comes back very quickly.

Interactive Finance Services may be found at *http://www.loancorp.co.uk/*

Money World

The list of companies advertising on this site is very impressive indeed. Bradford and Bingley, Scottish Widows, Legal and General and Eagle Star to name but a few.

The Money World site contains an amazing amount of material including a financial jargon buster where just about every banking and finance term is explained in clear, easy-to-understand language.

 This site is for information only and does not constitute advice within the terms of the FSA 1986.

You can also use this site to find out the current performance (for saving and borrowing) of all sorts of financial services.

One of the most useful areas of this site is the section offering help for homebuyers.

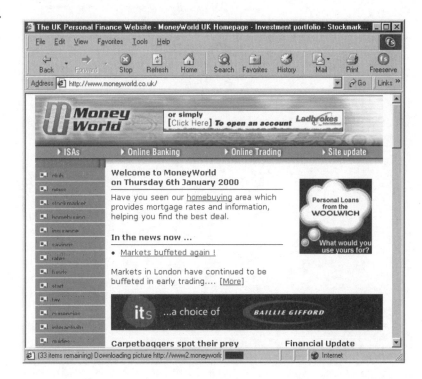

Money World is at *http://www.moneyworld.co.uk/*

Also worth visiting is EM Finance at *http:// www.emfinance.com/*

Nationwide

The Nationwide site is packed with current information about its services.

Online banking is its latest offering and there is a link on the site to enable you to apply for this service. As outlined previously, this facility is particularly useful for regularly keeping track of your bank accounts.

Nationwide is also an Internet Service Provider and as long as you have a Nationwide bank account you can also enjoy the ISP services offered.

For followers of the British Football League, this is a great place to get the latest information.

The Nationwide website includes a useful section on financial planning which is well worth reading.

As the Nationwide sponsors the Football League, there is also a section on the League with information about most of the clubs in the top divisions. You can also view the Football League table.

Nationwide is at *http://www.nationwide.co.uk/*

Universal Currency Converter

This is a clever and very useful site. Simply, it will convert an input sum of money from almost any currency into another. Begin by entering the amount of money to be converted. Next, choose the currency you want to convert from, and the one to convert to. Finally, click on the Convert button at the bottom of the page. The current exchange rates will be applied to the sum of money entered, and the result will be output on the next page.

If you have a portable computer, this is a handy site to access whilst on holiday.

Although the conversions are accurate, there is a disclaimer stating that accuracy is not guaranteed.

The Universal Currency Converter is at *http://www.xe.net/ currency*.

Other financial sites

Xest

Execution only electronic share trading – delivers stock market information, analysis and the ability to initiate transactions. Xest is at *http://www.xest.com/*

Online Banking Report

A visit to *http://www.netbanker.com/* will provide you with exclusive monthly reports on home banking and interactive financial products.

My Bank

My Bank at *http://www.mybank.com/* provides a comprehensive directory to help you locate banks on the Internet.

Beware of sites that guarantee a quick profit.

CBS Market Watch

Keep an eye on the world share market at *http://cbs.marketwatch.com/*

Investorama

Everything you need for playing the stock market is at *http://www.investorama.com/*

Her Money

http://www.hermoney.co.uk/ provides jargon-free information for women about managing money.

Morgan Stanley Dean Witter

Real time 24 hour bond trading is just one of the services offered online at *http://www.online.msdw.com/*

Smart Money

Visit *http://www.smartmoney.com/* and it will tell you how best to invest your money.

Foreign Exchange Rates

All the latest prices from the world's markets are at *http://quotes.reuters.com/*

Virtual Trading

If you don't want to play for real, play the Global Strategist Game at *http://www.global-strategist.com/*

Internet shopping

Like Internet banking, shopping on the Internet has a mixed press. Some see it as a dream come true, others as little more than a gimmick which wastes more time than it saves.

Covers

Chapter Fourteen

IKEA

I remember reading the instructions that came with a flat-packed wardrobe. It had been translated into English from, presumably, Italian (since that was where the product was made). Judging by the result, it was evident that the person who did the translation was conversant in neither language. The quality of the product was commensurate with the instructions, and about as much thought had gone into the design of the instructions as the furniture. How things have changed.

For those whose fashion consciousness extends to the home, IKEA is the place to go. There are numerous shops both in the UK and overseas.

 This is a useful site to visit if you're redesigning a room.

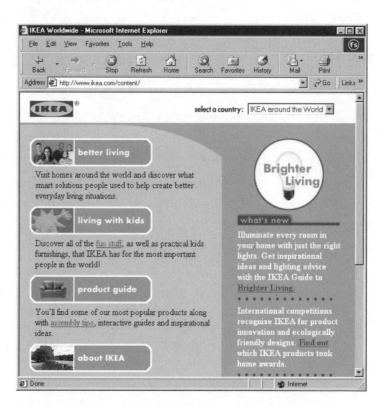

This site has several useful sections, including 'living with kids' which gives some useful tips for furnishing children's rooms. IKEA can be found at *http://www.ikea.com/*

The Body Shop

Using animals for testing medicines that will eventually save lives is one thing, but using animals for testing make-up so that women (and men) can make themselves appear more attractive is something else.

The thousands of people who agree have made the Body Shop the success that it has been.

This is not so much a shopping site as a website about the shop. The name Body Shop has become synonymous with fair trade, natural products and non-animal testing.

For lovers of Body Shop products, this site provides a wealth of information about them, about the company itself and its trade links.

This is an excellent site to use in schools.

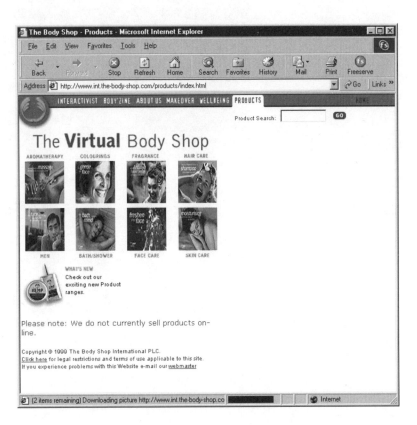

The Body Shop site is at *http://www.bodyshop.com/*

Racing Green

Racing Green is part of the Arcadia Group which includes Burton and Dorothy Perkins. Their website shows all of their products available through mail order and also includes online ordering.

Ensure you order the correct size and colour for each item you order.

Have your credit card handy.

Once an order is started, each page gives you an opportunity to add to your virtual shopping basket. The bill is totalled for you and secure credit card payment is available.

The Racing Green website is at *www.racinggreen.co.uk/*

Next

Staying with fashion, the Next website offers the user an online catalogue showing many of the Next products. Originally offering fashion clothes for those who no longer qualify for a Club 18–30 holiday, Next now sell accessories and a range of stylish household products and children's clothes.

Keep a look out for online ordering.

Although online shopping is not yet available, you can order a catalogue by completing the online form. You'll be invoiced for £3.

The Next website is at *http://www.next.co.uk/*

Fashion clothes shopping

For some people, shopping for clothes is like an extended holiday and the ultimate retail therapy. Personally, I can't think of anything worse than queuing up at changing rooms, being badgered by commission-hungry sales assistants and then having to haul several heavy bags home on an overcrowded train. If you feel the same, Kingshill have the answer.

You don't need to leave your armchair to shop here.

You can't try things on if you buy on the Internet, but you can send them back if they don't fit.

Kingshill offer clothes from several top fashion names which you can browse through from the comfort of your own armchair. It's not dissimilar to strolling through a shop. Just click on a fashion name and look through the collection.

You don't have to be a member to view the site, but you do need to register to make a purchase.

Go to *http://www.kingshill.co.uk/* to get to Kingshill's front page. You can order a catalogue for £3 and once registered you can shop without leaving your home.

...cont'd

There are several brand names in this store.

You can wander through several top design names and place items in your virtual shopping basket. When you've finished, take your virtual shopping basket to the virtual check-out where the items you've purchased will be totalled and you'll be billed on your non-virtual credit card.

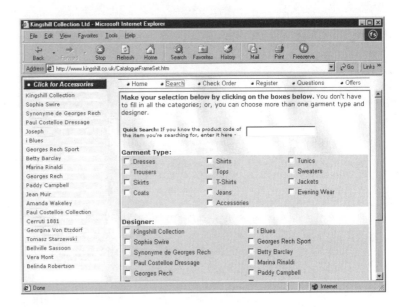

Sainsbury's

With an emphasis on quality at reassuringly low prices, Sainsbury's has been a feature of high streets for as long as I can remember.

One of my earliest memories was waiting outside Sainsbury's whilst Mum was shopping. At that time, Sainsbury's was a shop rather than a supermarket and they frequently had goods on marble tables in the window. Eggs were most common and they were arranged according to quality. A big sign spelt it out, 'Best English New-Laid Eggs'. Next to that, 'English New-Laid Eggs'. On the next table, 'New Laid Eggs', and right at the end it simply read, 'Eggs'.

The Sainsbury's site also contains links to other shops in the chain.

More and more supermarkets are opening websites and offering customers the chance to shop online. Try to find your nearest supermarket.

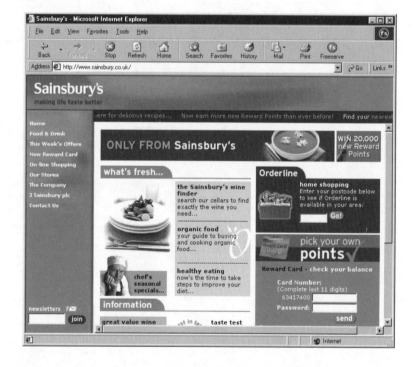

The Sainsbury's website offers customers the chance to order online but also gives other value-added features such as recipes and information about the Sainsbury reward card scheme.

Sainsbury's are at *http://www.sainsbury.co.uk/*

Homebase

Homebase is Sainsbury's 'do-it-yourself' shop. Although you can't actually shop at this site, you can wander around and get some ideas for improvements for both house and garden. There are details about the Homebase 'Spend and Save Card' as well as seasonal tips to brighten up your home and garden.

If you're stuck for decorating ideas, look no further.

There is a useful list of products with a description to give you an idea of what is available before trudging off to buy it. If you don't happen to have a Homebase in downtown Sydney, it is still useful as it gives a list of tools, some of which you might not know exist, and which may be at your local DIY store.

The section on choosing gifts is a particularly interesting and useful one aimed at people who, like me, never quite know what to buy for a birthday present.

Visit Homebase at *http://www.homebase.co.uk/*

ASDA

Originally Associated Dairies, now part of the giant Wal Mart, ASDA are currently advertising quality and value and this is reflected in their website. The site includes the week's top 20 offers and regularly updated recipes, including meals for people with special dietary requirements.

There are several screens of information about calories, their consumption and how to cut down on them.

ASDA is at *http://www.asda.com/*

Check out this site every week to take advantage of the best offers.

There are ASDA jobs advertised on this site.

In association with ASDA, Value Mad is a shopping site where they seem to offer anything and everything. You can even get a quote for an electricity supply from them.

Everything from books to mobile phones is on offer at significantly reduced prices. You can visit Value Mad at *http://www.valuemad.com/*

Traidcraft

Traidcraft is an organisation which trades with workers in developing countries and imports their products for sale in this country.

What makes Traidcraft stand out is that it deals fairly with the workers and pays them a sensible wage for the work they have done.

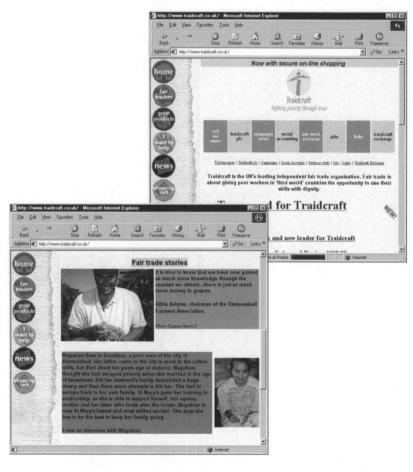

Although some products may be slightly more expensive, they have been traded fairly.

In short, the people of developing countries are not being exploited to provide goods so that we in the developed world can buy more of the products at lower prices.

You can now order online from Traidcraft, whose website is at *http://www.traidcraft.co.uk/*

The Shopping Zone

This is probably the definitive website for information about Web shopping. The Shopping Zone lists most shops that offer online shopping and rates them according to which services they offer.

Details about secure payments are listed and other services are given a star rating.

Make sure credit card payment is through a secure connection.

The information about online services is thoughtfully divided into categories such as banks, bookshops, computers, department stores, music, fashion and videos.

The Shopping Zone is at *http://shopping.lineone.net/*

Dixons

Comparing prices on the Web is much easier than trudging around shops.

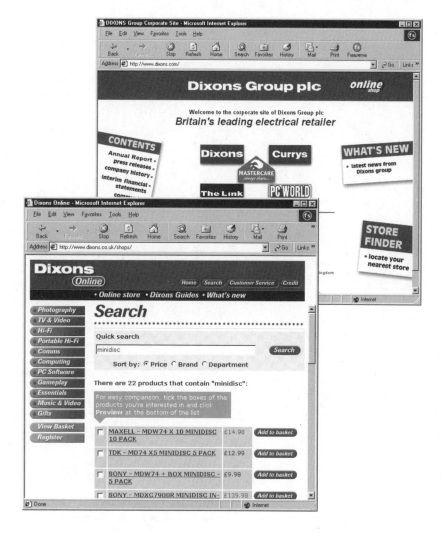

Of all the online shopping sites, this seems to be one of the easiest to use. On the first page you're asked to choose the overall category of product you wish to purchase (computer, hi-fi, portable hi-fi, communications etc.). You then select a specific item within that category.

Further information on each product is available before deciding whether to purchase online.

Dixons are at *http://www.dixons.co.uk/*

Other shopping sites

A bargain

Buy an Internet domain name from *http://www.abargain.com/*

Interflora

Say it with flowers without having to go into the garden to cut them yourself. Interflora are at *http://www.interflora.com/*

Let's buy it

This site sounds more like the anthem my children sing when we go shopping. Visit *http://www.letsbuyit.com/* for some bargains.

You must have a credit card to use these sites effectively.

Freeshop

If you like getting freebies visit *http://www.freeshop.com/* for great products from all around the Web – each with something for free. Choose from free shipping, personalisation, buy-one-get-one-free and more!

Roboshopper

This site compares prices using a powerful search engine. For the best bargains, *http://www.roboshopper.com/*

Computer shopper

Go to *http://shopper.cnet.com/* to search out the best computer bargains. Also includes printers, cameras – in fact, almost anything that has a chip in it.

Food and drink

For some, food is so much more than just fuel to keep going. If you want to find out more about the food you eat, or you just want a new recipe to try out on your friends, the Internet is the place to go.

Covers

Chapter Fifteen

Meat matters

Meat in general, and British meat in particular, has had its fair share of bad publicity. Recent scares about the safety of meat and meat products have made us all question the meat industry.

This site gives an insight into the meat industry for both consumers and those who work in it.

Check out the meat recipes on this site.

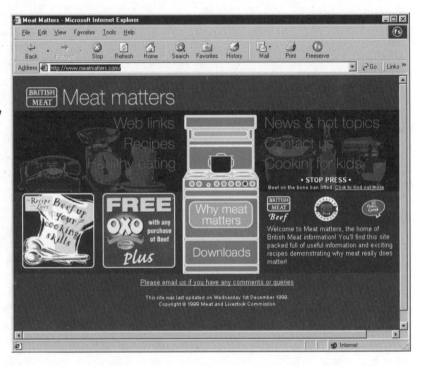

For many visitors to this site, the main route from the title page will be to the excellent recipes using favourite cuts of lamb, beef and pork. I can't claim to have tried them all, but those I have are excellent.

Like many good websites, the 'Meat matters' site has a page of links to other sites. In this case, the links are to other good food sites.

The 'Meat matters' website may be found at *http://www.meatmatters.com/*

Boddington's beer

This site contains a handy screensaver to download.

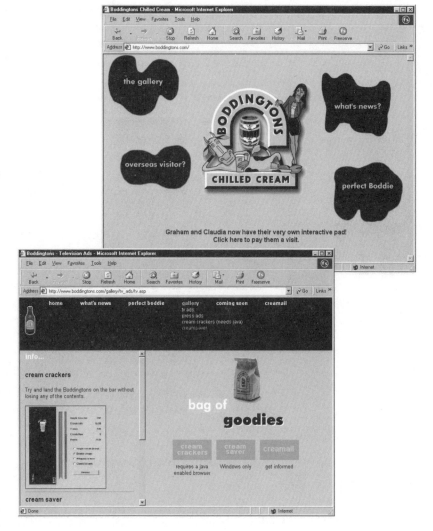

The brewers of the beer dubbed the 'Cream of Manchester' have a particularly light-hearted site providing all manner of snippets about their beer.

One of the highlights is a screensaver which can be downloaded and used on your computer.

The Cream of Websites may be found at *http://www. boddingtons.com/*

Cheese

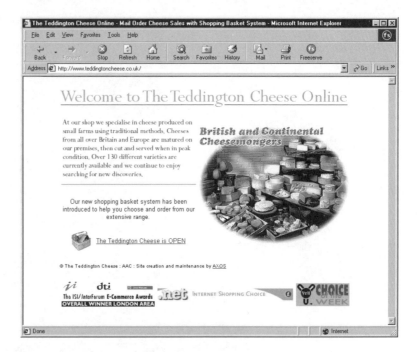

You can order online from this site.

For connoisseurs of fine cheese, this is the place to come. Teddington Cheese have over 130 varieties of fine cheeses from around the world, which can be ordered online if required. There are descriptions of cheeses and some suggestions for cheeseboards.

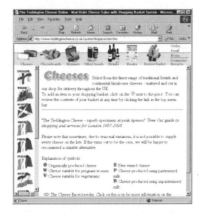

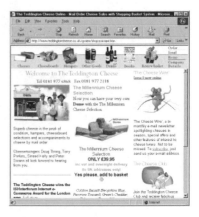

Teddington Cheese Online may be found at *http://www. teddingtoncheese.co.uk/*

Wine

It's not always easy to find a wine you really like. I find that some really cheap wines are very good while some expensive wines, to me, taste like vinegar.

 The best wine to buy is the one you like.

For lovers of fine wine, the Wine Spectator website is the place to visit. This site is crammed full of information about fine wines for both the expert and the novice.

The Wine Spectator is at *http://www.winespectator.com/*

Eating at home

Domino's Pizza

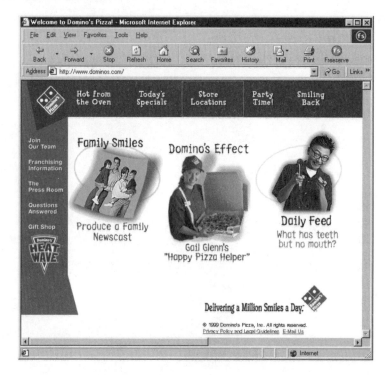

You can order online from this site.

I've found the box often tastes better than the contents of many home-delivered pizzas. Domino's, on the other hand, produce an excellent range of 'custom-made' pizzas which are cooked to perfection and don't taste like oil-soaked cardboard.

The Domino's website contains news about the chain of outlets as well as giving you information about becoming a franchisee – a lucrative occupation, I understand. There are some games to play (most of which have a pizza connection) and there's the chance to join the Domino's Pizza Club.

Their websites at *http://www.dominos.com/* (for US residents) and *http://www.dominos.co.uk/* (for UK residents) have an online ordering service. To help you order your pizza, there's a store locator and a menu to enable you to 'design' your own pizza.

Ben and Jerry's Ice Cream

What better after a pizza than some ice cream? The trouble with much of the commercial ice cream is that its manufacture doesn't even include milk, let alone cream. Ice cream dates back to Victorian times when it was made from cream and fruit, and then frozen by placing it in a mould which was turned in ice.

Ben and Jerry's ice cream is much the same, except that the freezing process is a little more in keeping with the 21st Century.

In addition to information about the ice cream, including details of their latest flavour, there are games to be played and some fun activities for the kids.

This ice cream is addictive!

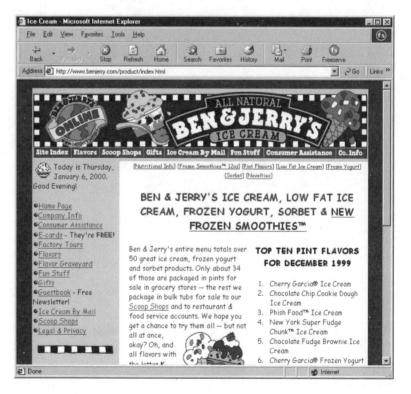

Ben and Jerry's ice cream website may be found at *http://www.benjerry.com/*

More TV snacks

The Real Thing

Coca-Cola is the best known brand worldwide. Hardly surprising when you see the red and white logo emblazoned across anything and everything.

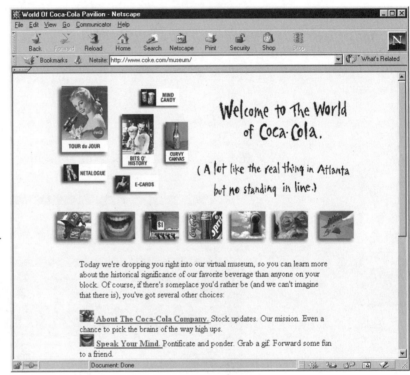

Always brush your teeth after consuming drinks containing sugar.

Apart from the removal of one ingredient, the recipe has hardly changed since its launch to US soldiers over half a century ago. Coca-Cola continues to go from strength to strength in spite of stories about the effects on teeth and the inside of your stomach.

The website is full of information about the drink and about the company, including its sponsorship of sport. In fact, everything about the Coca-Cola brand is here.

The Coca-Cola website which is at *http://www.coke.com/* has frequently been voted best website.

Walkers Crisps

I tend to restrict the number of packets of crisps in the house as I've found the children start grazing on them. If they're a little bored, they pop off to the pantry and emerge chomping on a bag of crisps. An hour later they don't want any dinner.

This of course is entirely understandable – crisps are very moreish.

This is about the most expensive way of buying potatoes.

The Walkers Crisps website gives a fascinating insight into what has become the most popular brand of potato crisp on sale.

Not only does it cover the traditional potato crisp, but also the other products in the Walkers range.

There are several games to be played, all of which have a crisp theme, and there is lots of information about the Qubix – the jigsaw pieces that are given away inside the packets.

Walkers crisps are at *http://www.walkers.co.uk/*

Chocolate

Cadbury's Chocolate

Chocaholics will love this. I immediately put on 2 pounds just smelling it.

Chocolate was first used by the Aztecs, although it was very bitter compared to chocolate bought today. The process by which chocolate is made is a long and fascinating one. Not to mention scientific.

Chocaholics may find these sites difficult to avoid.

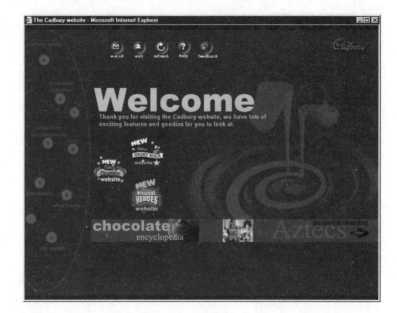

Cadbury is probably the best known chocolate in this country. Their website is at *http://www.cadbury.co.uk/* and is a particularly interesting site. Rather than just outlining their products, this site gives a vast amount of information about the history of chocolate, where it is grown, the modern manufacturing process and its distribution.

There is an education section, which is well worth visiting, and a recruitment section.

Apart from its use as a confection, chocolate is also a cooking ingredient and Cadbury have included a recipe section which contains some truly mouthwatering recipes.

Godiva's World of Chocolate
Continuing the waist-expanding theme, the World of Chocolate website by Godiva details their range of high-quality chocolates with mouthwatering illustrations. Godiva are at *http://www.godiva.com/*

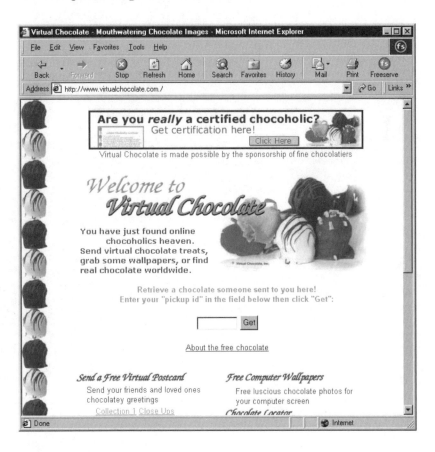

Virtual Chocolates are less fattening than real ones.

Virtual Chocolates
You can also use the Web to send someone a virtual chocolate. If you're not sure what that is, go to *http://www.virtualchocolate.com/*

Chocnet
Real chocolates can be ordered from Chocnet at *http://orders.mkn.co.uk/choc/.en*

Coffee

We seem to take so much for granted. A cup of coffee arrives at our desk and we swill it down without a second thought. Yet the route from the bean to the cup is a long and fascinating one.

Like wine, there is a lot of nonsense talked about coffee. This site will help sort out the truth.

The Coffee World website offers an insight into the production of coffee and includes a huge number of facts about it. The map shows where most of the world's coffee is grown and gives an explanation of the different types and blends available.

The Coffee World website may be visited at *http://www. realcoffee.co.uk/* where there is an online ordering service.

The Coffee.com website is similar in content and may be found at *http://www.coffee.com/*

Jam

I was well into my 20's before I tasted shop-bought jam. My grandfather used to swear that shop-bought raspberry jam contained sawdust to simulate the pips. So, my grandmother used to make it. The recipe was simple: it contained fruit and sugar and nothing else.

Not all jam is made in the same way as grandmother's.

Whilst not containing doubtful ingredients such as sawdust, many modern shop-bought jams contain a great deal more than fruit and sugar. Tiptree export their jam to the far corners of the earth and the Tiptree website clearly demonstrates how their jam has hardly changed over the years. Information includes fruit growing, the company itself and tourist information.

Tiptree jams are at *http://www.tiptree.com/*

Other tasty sites

Tea
If you like tea, you'll find this site thoroughly enjoyable. Clipper Teas are at *http://www.clipper-teas.co.uk/*

Cocktails
http://hotwired.lycos.com/cocktail/ contains recipes for cocktails, and some amusing anecdotes to go with them. The advice here, though, is to print out the recipe and mix the drink away from the computer.

Drinks Direct
For all your alcoholic needs, including gifts for friends, visit Drinks Direct at *http://www.drinks-direct.co.uk/*

Epicurious Food
http://food.epicurious.com/ is packed full of ideas, tips for buying food, recipes and features by top chefs.

There are countless food and drink websites. These are just a few of the best.

You won't need a can opener if you buy from these sites.

Farmshop Directory
If you believe that potatoes come out of a packet and not out of the ground, then visit the Farmshop Directory at *http://www.farmshop.net/directory/start.asp*

...cont'd

FruitNet UK

For lovers of fresh fruit which can be ordered direct from several countries, FruitNet UK is at *http://orders.mkn.co.uk/fruit/.en.*

Heinz

The famous 57 varieties of Heinz can be explored at their website at *http://www.heinz.co.uk/*

Although some of these sites are aimed at a specific market, most have information relevant to other markets.

Whilst the site exists primarily to advertise their products, it does contain important nutritional information and some interesting history about the brand. Corporate details are available at *http://www.heinz.com/*

Honey

Everything you ever wanted to know about honey is at *http://www.honey.com/*

There is also a link to the National Honey Board which details the differences between honeys and has links to other useful sites.

The Internet Chef

Probably the most comprehensive culinary website. Hundreds of recipes, kitchen chat, recipe of the week – it's all here at *http://www.ichef.com/*

Kelloggs

I'm sure their slogan must be true – if it doesn't say Kelloggs on the box, it isn't Kelloggs in the box. For some reason, they do taste better than other brands. Kelloggs Cereals' website is at *http://www.kelloggs.com/*

Magnum Fine Wines

Magnum Fine Wines at *http://www.magnum.co.uk/* is about buying wine to keep as an investment. If you want a couple of bottles of cheap plonk to swill back with your curry, look elsewhere.

Moet & Chandon

Whenever I see a bottle of Moet & Chandon (which actually isn't that often) I'm always reminded of the song by Queen in which the opening line is, 'She drinks Moet & Chandon from a pretty cabinet...'. Why not a glass? Find out more about the queen of champagnes at *http://www.moet.com/*

Moonshine

Distilling spirit is illegal in some countries.

If your country allows spirit distilling, then *http://www. moonshine.co.nz/* can provide you with recipes and even the kit to make it. But beware, this stuff can be really powerful so always stop drinking when you see four or more computer monitors in front of you.

Müller

The thought of cold rice pudding is enough to make anyone feel full. But call it cool dairy rice, put it into a fancy pot with some fruit and you've got a winner. But Müller rice *is* a very enjoyable dessert. Their website is *http:// www.muller.co.uk/*

Mushrooms

Make sure you know what you're doing before gathering wild 'mushrooms'.

If you think mushroom growers are solitary beings who spend most of their time in the dark, then log onto Mushroomers at *http://members.aol.com/basidium/mushpepl.html* to get the record put straight. It details every type of mushroom, and has links to several other sites.

Organics Direct

Organic food is easy to spot in a supermarket – it's usually brown and always more expensive. To find out why this is, and to learn of the benefits, visit Organics Direct at *http://www.organicsdirect.com/*

Pringles

There are lots of sites with recipes; none seem to be guaranteed to work, although most do.

Potato crisps always used to be different sizes. This was due to the fact that potatoes come in different sizes. Pringles have overcome this inherent defect and produce perfectly formed, identical crisps that fit into a tube. The website at *http://www.pringles.com/* is great fun and well worth a visit.

Smoked salmon

For lovers of Scottish smoked salmon, the Shetland Smokehouse website at *http://www.shetlandseafood.co.uk/* shows you how it's done. You can order food online and even have it delivered as a present.

Spices

Spice Advice at *http://www.spiceguide.com/* is a definitive guide to the origins of spices and their use in cooking. The Spice encyclopedia is essential reading.

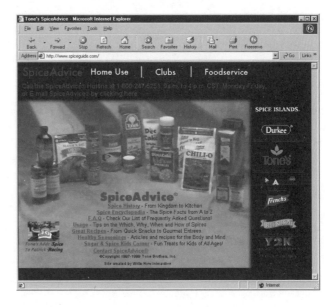

Sugar

The Sugar Information Service at *http://www.sugarinfo.co.uk/* provides all the facts about the product we're being told to consume less of.

Brush your teeth well after eating sugar or sticky sweets.

Traditional sweets

Traditional sweets have not disappeared but are still being produced. Visit *http://www.sela.co.uk/* to find out where you can buy humbugs, cough candy and other throat-incinerating confectionery.

Tia Maria

The coffee liqueur's website at *http://www.tiamaria.co.uk/* contains some interesting material – and not just about their drink. If viewing this page you'll need a very good monitor as the print is about the smallest I've ever seen.

Fizzy Pop

Although many of these sites are produced for commercial purposes, they do contain some valuable information.

I can remember Seven-Up when I was a boy. I don't believe it's changed much since then. The Seven-Up website contains all the information about the product and who makes it. Also some online games to play. It can take a long time to load this site, but it will be worth it. Seven-Up is at *http://www.7up.com/*

Also try Tizer at *http://www.tizer.co.uk/*

Van den Bergh Foods

This is the parent company of such well known products as OXO, PG Tips, Colemans, Flora and Chicken Tonight. To find out more, visit *http://www.vdbfoods.co.uk/*

Wine Net

Wine Net at *http://wine.net/* is a guide for lovers of good wines from around the world. This site has links to vineyards and retailers.

Somerfield and KwikSave

These famous stores' website contains recipes, quick meals and a special section for the kids at *http://www.somerfield.co.uk/*

Healthy living

We eat too much, drink too much, eat the wrong things and we don't take enough exercise. Oh yes, and we spend too much time in front of computers. We are not a healthy race!

The Internet can provide some help, but before ploughing on with a list of sites to increase longevity, a few words of caution. It has long been recognised that giving a layman a medical book with which to carry out self-diagnosis is not always sound. If you really think something is wrong, it's best to seek qualified medical advice.

Covers

Chapter Sixteen

Women's health

Ask a Woman Doctor

Go to these sites for help and advice about female health issues.

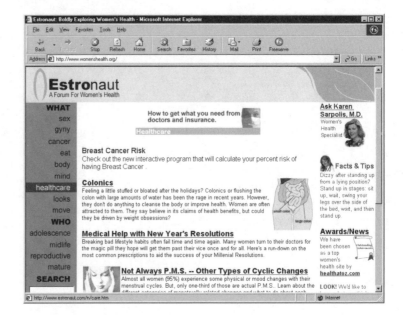

There is no shortage of help specifically aimed at women on the Web. The Ask a Woman Doctor website offers women a range of information provided by doctors. Subjects include sexual issues, including contraception, as well as a range of matters relating to PMT and the menopause. Ask a Woman Doctor can be found at *http://www.womenshealth.org/*

Women's Nutritional Advisory Service

The Women's Nutritional Advisory Service is at *http://www. wnas.org.uk/* For an alternative approach to helping with health problems, try *http://www.weleda. co.uk/*

Ask Anna

Http://www.askanna.co.uk/ is billed as the relationship Internet site for women. This site aims to offer women intelligent, sympathetic and non-judgemental advice on relationship issues, by famous columnist Anna Raeburn. Included in the site is a chat room, 'find a friend' and real life stories.

Tampax

The Tampax website exists primarily to promote their products but goes much further by providing forums on a variety of women's issues.

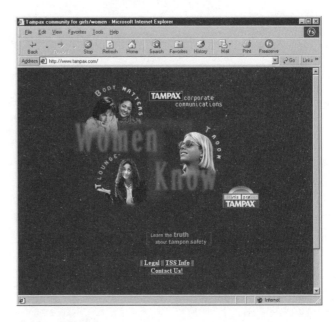

Although this is a commercial site, it does contain some very helpful information.

There have been some concerns about the safety of tampons and there is a section which places the facts at your disposal.

The homepage has links to other Tampax related sites – TLounge is a forum for women to discuss issues and Body Matters is, as the name suggests, about promoting health.

There is also the opportunity to get some free samples by clicking on the link and entering your name and address in the space provided.

The Tampax site is at *http://www.tampax.com/*

Virtual Checkup

If you feel in need of a checkup it's best to visit your doctor, but in the interim try *http:// www.allhealth.com/virtualcheckup/*

National Osteoporosis Society

Osteoporosis is the thinning of the bones which usually begins after the menopause. The National Osteoporosis Society (*http://www.nos.org.uk/*) will provide women with help and advice.

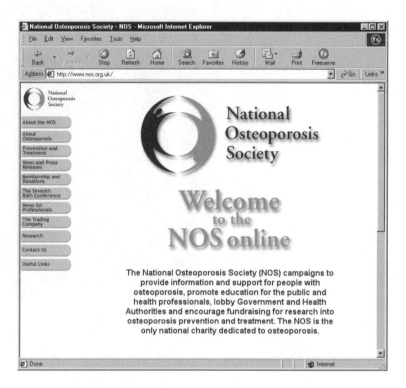

The list of headings on the front page shows some of the issues covered by this very valuable and well constructed site.

Progesterone cream

Seek advice before using medication.

The site claims that in a three year study of post-menopausal osteoporosis patients, women who used natural progesterone cream actually increased bone density by an average of 8% in the first year, by 4% in the second year and 2% in subsequent years, against the USA national average of a 1.5% annual loss. Natural Progesterone Cream is also claimed to provide relief from PMT. The site is at *http:// www.progesterone.co.uk/*

British Pregnancy Advisory Service

This site also provides advice about abortions and vasectomy.

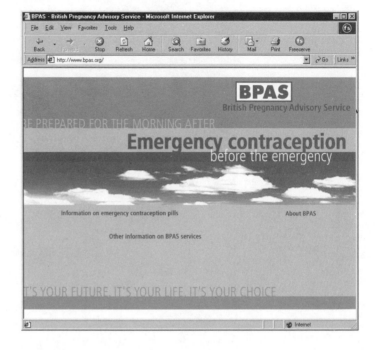

Although a British site, much of this information is relevant to women from all countries.

The British Pregnancy Advisory Service doesn't just provide help and advice about pregnancy. Included in this site is a wealth of information about how not to become pregnant and dealing with an unwanted pregnancy. The BPAS website may be found at *http://www.bpas.org/*

http://www.babyworld.co.uk/ was set up for women as the Internet parenting site. It is aimed at new and expectant mothers where they can learn about their bodies, their baby and childbirth, and celebrate the joy of new life.

http://www.feelgooduk.co.uk/ is an instant and confidential source of in-depth, up-to-date and expert information and advice on women's health issues. The site includes information about common female problems and sexual health, and also a chat room and contraception advice.

Men's health

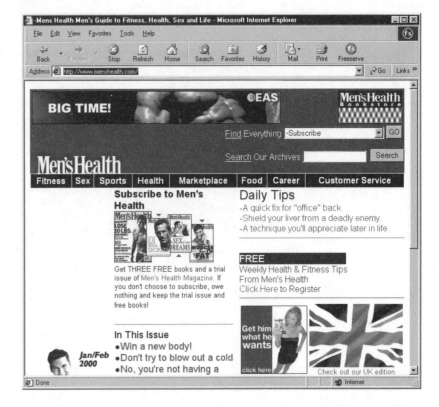

Go to these sites for help and advice about male health issues.

Like women, men too have their fair share of health problems. Men's Health is a monthly magazine which offers help and advice to men about their health. This is now available on the Internet as a monthly online magazine.

This website is at *http://www.menshealth.com/*

Viagra

The male anti-impotence drug Viagra must be the best known drug since aspirin. Certainly, I can't remember a drug receiving so much attention, even before it was launched. For men suffering with impotence, a visit to *http://www.viagra.com/* might put them onto the right path.

Healthgate

Healthgate is another site offering advice for male problems, although it also offers advice for women and children. Regularly updated, Healthgate addresses all the major issues which men seem uneasy about discussing with their GP.

There is an excellent search facility here and it can be found at *http://www.healthgate.com/*

If in doubt, seek medical advice.

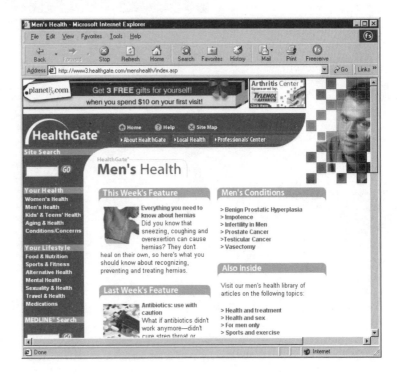

Condoms are more than just contraceptives.

Condoms

Apart from their contraceptive use, a condom will prevent the spread of sexually transmitted diseases. Some men use them as a matter of course, others can't seem to manage them. Whichever category you fit into, *http://www.condom.com/* will take you to the site for more information.

Probably the most famous of all brands of condom is Durex and their site is at *http://www.durex.com/*

Men's Fitness

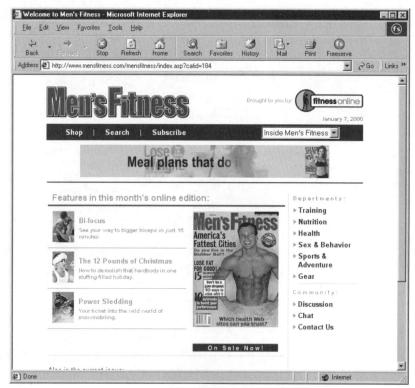

This site contains lots of healthy advice – read it carefully.

Although fitness is not just a male issue, this site is concerned only with male fitness. As can be seen from the home page, it covers not only muscle building but also nutrition and lifestyle – both of which contribute very significantly to our overall health.

The site does not shy away from any issue, and yet it never degenerates into foul or inappropriate language. Everything is covered in a plain and simple style which is easily accessible.

Regular features include Sex & Behavior, Training and Nutrition.

Visit this site at *http://www.mensfitness.com/*

Men's sexual issues

A recent survey found that men are far less likely to seek medical advice, especially when it's a sexual or bowel problem. As a result, thousands of men are dying, literally through embarrassment. For those who do find it difficult to talk about these matters, this site might help you change your mind.

You must type the address exactly as given.

It deals with sexual issues such as premature ejaculation and testicular self-examination.

Slightly 'offbeat' in its approach, it contains some vital hints and advice for keeping the lower regions in order.

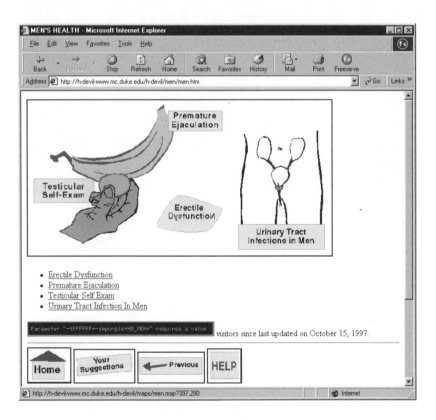

To visit this site, enter *http://h-devil-www.mc.duke.edu/h-devil/men/men.htm*

Cancer

Cancer can affect everyone – young or old, black or white, male or female. Having witnessed the effects, not only on the patient but also on the family, I know only too well what it can do.

For the patient, there is medical help, but it's often the families that also need help and support.

The Cancer website is at *http://medweb.bham.ac.uk/cancerhelp/public/orgs/useorgs.html*

Support for the family is often as important as for the patient.

CancerBACUP (note the spelling) recognises the need for family support, has lots of practical advice to offer and will point patients and carers in the right direction.

If you are suffering from cancer, or a member of your family has cancer, go to *http://www.cancerbacup.org.uk/*

The following three cancers claim a great many lives – too many – and regular checks can reduce the possibility of surgery. Although these websites are all UK-based, they contain a great deal of valuable information for women of all countries.

Regular checks will help reduce the possibility of surgery.

Breast Cancer

In the UK, if you're a woman over 50, you'll be invited to get a free mammogram. Other countries have different arrangements, including no arrangements whatsoever. Either way, it's worth checking out *http://www.breastcancerfund.org/*

If in doubt, seek medical advice.

Cervical Cancer

A regular smear test will help detect this cancer. Find out more by going to *http://www.nccc-online.org/*

Ovarian Cancer

Jenny Agutter is the Patron of Ovacome. Their website is at *http://www.ovacome.org.uk/*

If you're considering donating to a charity, consider one of these.

Cancer Charities

The Macmillan website is at *http://www.macmillan.org.uk/* and The Marie Curie website is at *http://www.mariecurie.org.uk/*

Prostate cancer

Early diagnosis is beneficial. Regular checks will help.

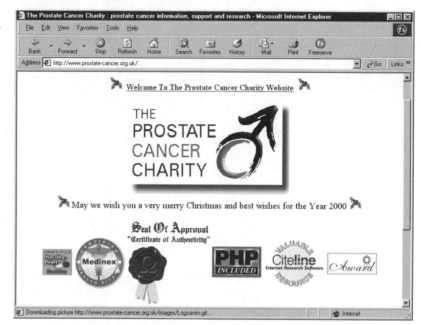

Prostate cancer is the most common male cancer, and has the highest mortality. Yet this cancer is often curable if caught in time. The trouble seems to be that men are just too shy or embarrassed to discuss the matter and so it gets left until it's too late. Find out more about prostate cancer at *http://www.prostate-cancer.org.uk/*

Testicular cancer

The other scourge of the male population is testicular cancer. Again, it need not be fatal if treated in time. For more information go to *http://www.orchid-cancer.org.uk/*

Alternative approaches

Many people, including some doctors, believe that alternative or complementary medicine has a place in the treatment of cancer. The New Approaches to Cancer is a registered charity and their website at *http://www.anac. org.uk/* advocates positive self-help as part of the treatment.

Smoking

Quit smoking

As an ex-smoker, I'm amazed that anyone should want to start today. Since stopping over 15 years ago, I'm fitter and generally healthier. I've also saved a fortune.

 It's also worth reading the health warning on cigarette packets.

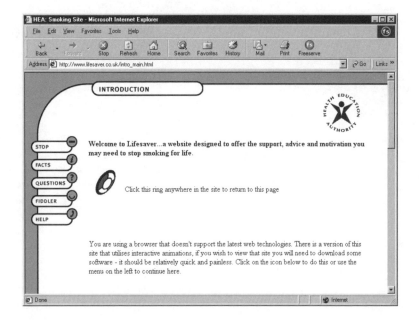

Giving up cigarettes isn't easy, and the longer you've been smoking the harder it is.

 Non-smokers get better rates for life insurance.

But it is possible, although it does take willpower and not just a quick visit to this site. Many will find chewing gum, patches and even alternative treatments like acupuncture helpful.

Once at this site you'll find practical advice as well as numerous facts about the effects of smoking so that if you were in any doubt about it, you won't be after reading it.

Personally, I found that any positive step towards stopping was a step in the right direction.

The Quit Smoking site can be found by going to (appropriately) *http://www.lifesaver.co.uk/*

Hay fever

Fortunately I don't suffer with hay fever, although I know several people who do. They have a miserable time of it when the pollen count is high.

To find out more about hay fever, go to *http://medical-legal.co.uk/patient_info/allergy.htm.*

Use these sites to find ways of learning to live with hay fever and migraine.

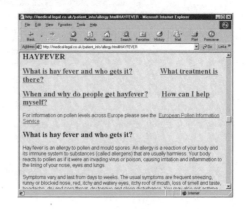

Migraine

A headache can be bad, but migraine is quite different. For those millions who, like me, suffer with migraines, any help which is available will be welcome. This site offers practical help for sufferers so they may at least learn to live with migraine. Visit the migraine site at *http://www.migraine.org.uk/*

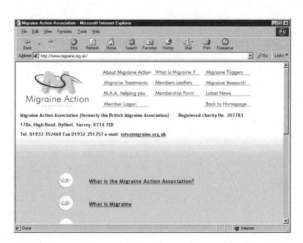

Biorhythms

The theory is, that when you are born, three cycles begin: Physical, Emotional and Intellectual. The duration of each of the cycles is different, but their duration is known and so if you enter your birthday and the present day, it's a relatively simple piece of maths to calculate the state of your being now, or at any particular time.

Some people claim that the critical time is when the waves cross the centre line, others claim that above the line (+) means you're in good form, whilst below the line means things are likely not to go quite as well in that particular arena.

Some people take these very seriously.

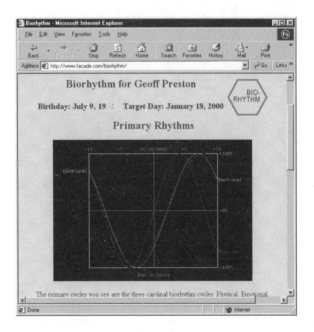

Some people take these very seriously to the extent of planning their lives around them. Some even go to the extent of comparing their biorhythm with that of their partner and keeping clear of each other if both emotional rhythms are low or critical if they are crossing the centre line.

To find out more about Biorhythms, visit *http://www.facade.com/biorhythm/* where you can plot your own.

Other healthy sites

The Parents Place

Like most parents, I thought it would get easier. Not so. The older they get, the more grief children seem to generate. The Parents Place at *http://www.parentsplace.com/* is the place to go for answers to almost any question about parenting from conception onwards. It includes advice about fertility, caring for baby, breast feeding and even includes information about the health issues of the mum-to-be.

Yahoo lists lots of health-related websites.

Dr Greene's House Calls

This website covers a range of issues for each stage of child development up to and including adolescence, but not including the second childhood. There is also a wealth of information about issues that many people seem too embarrassed to talk about like bed-wetting, breast feeding and potty training. Dr Greene is at *http://www.drgreene.com/topic.html*

Health & Nursing

Health & Nursing lists all the usenet newsgroups that fall into the category of health and care. The site is at *http://www.shef.ac.uk/~nhcon/nunews.htm.*

...cont'd

Health Clinic

Health Clinic at *http://www.healthy.net/clinic/* offers visitors the opportunity to test 50 biological functions. There are also details about a vast range of ailments and afflictions ranging from acne to whooping cough. First aid information is also provided for an assortment of accidents and incidents from a dog-bite to sunburn.

Cardiopulmonary resuscitation

This could save someone's life. Learn the correct technique at *http://www.learncpr.org/*

This is not an alternative to proper medical training on CPR.

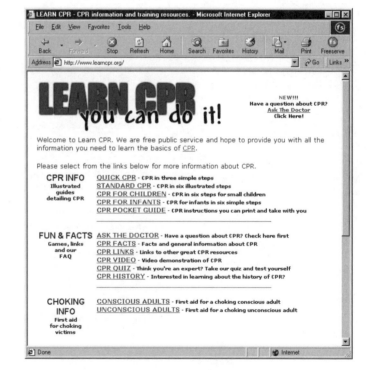

CPR can save lives if done correctly. If you don't do it correctly you could kill the patient anyway.

The Vegetarian Pages

A healthy diet is fundamental for a healthy body and some argue that the answer is vegetarianism. The Vegetarian Pages at *http://www.veg.org/* provides all the vital information, including recipes that use ingredients other than just beans and nuts.

Acupuncture

It is claimed that acupuncture has been successful for treating painful conditions such as arthritis, back pain and migraines. Research and practice over many years have shown acupuncture's effectiveness in helping a range of other conditions such as depression, asthma, hormonal problems and urinary disorders. To find out more, visit *http://www.flojo.demon.co.uk/*

Not all doctors agree that these alternative medicines work.

Homeopathy

The Queen of England is probably the most famous supporter of homeopathy. There are several homeopathic sites, but *http:/www.homeopathyhome.com/* and *http://www.efn.org/~cblack/homeopathy.html* seem about the best.

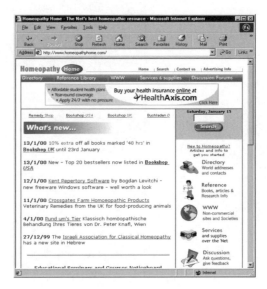

Pressures

Stress, anxiety, and psychological and emotional pressures affect all of us in our daily lives. Learn how to cope and deal with them at *http://www.stressfree.com/*

Amazing Surgeries

Witness actual operations online at *http://www. amazingsurgeries.com/*

Children's websites

The Internet can be an unsuitable place to leave children. Sadly, there is too much inappropriate material which children should not be subjected to. This chapter lists some websites that not only welcome children, but have been designed for the young, or the young at heart.

Covers

Chapter Seventeen

Argosphere

Interactive activities are not new to the Internet but those offered at Argosphere are consistently high-quality educational activities.

You'll need to register, so choose a password that your children will remember.

What Argosphere offers is a really well produced and safe site which kids (and adults) will enjoy strolling around. There are a variety of interactive tasks and exercises which can be either worked on online, or downloaded and used offline with any Java script Internet browser. (For most users that will be Internet Explorer or Netscape Communicator.)

The topics are diverse and sometimes slightly offbeat (like the Llama page, which contains just about everything you would want to know about Llamas).

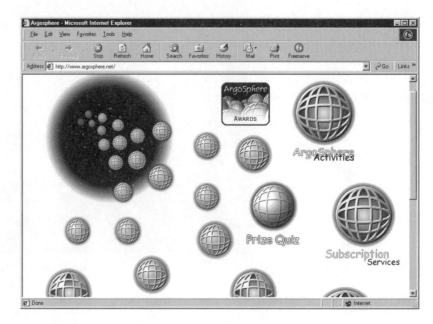

If you wish you can take part in a survey each time you log on to the site. Questions vary between which type of TV programme you most watch to whether we should buy goods from France.

There are also regular quizzes and additional information for parents and schools.

Most of the activities can be run offline which will reduce the phone bill.

There are a range of educational activities which will stimulate and educate. One section generates sums for children to work through. You can select the number range and the arithmetic signs used to suit your child. It will even produce an answer sheet for you.

All of the activities are age-related so that if, for example, you have an eight year old son or daughter, you will find a range of appropriate activities in the 8+ sphere.

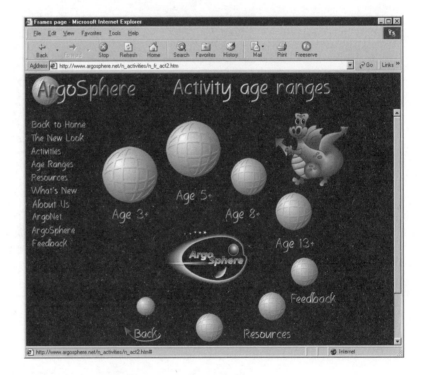

You will have to register the first time you use this site and you will need to provide a username and a password which will be required on each subsequent visit to the site.

Many of the activities are free although there is a charge for some. Full details of how to access the full site are available on the subscription page.

Connect to Argosphere at *http://www.argosphere.com/*

Star Tower

Star Tower was developed for Apple Xemplar by the same team that developed Argosphere and the format is similar: educational activities for a range of ages from the very young to early/mid teens. But if you're over 16, don't feel that this site need be avoided.

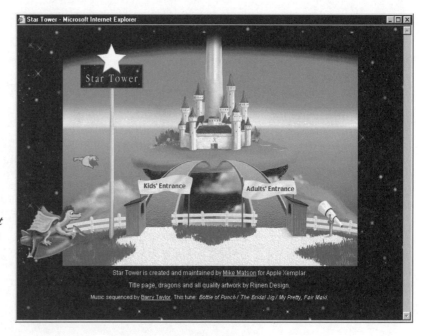

You need a fast modem or lots of patience to use this site.

Star Tower does take quite a long time to download as it uses some fairly large graphic files. But it's worth waiting for – the graphics are stunning and demonstrate what a browser is actually capable of doing.

The site is being constantly updated with ever more clever activities. Using the theme of a Star Tower to hold it all together, these activities are varied and suitable for a wide range of ages and abilities.

Download the activities and run them offline to reduce your phone bill.

As with Argosphere, all of the activities will run on any computer (Windows, Apple or Acorn) and the activities can be downloaded, saved onto disc and used offline. This means that you don't run up a phone bill whilst working out what you should do next.

For me, one of the highlights from this continuously developing site is the control activity featuring Unit the robot. You may choose from two activities (Apple Picking and Balloon Bursting) which involve providing Unit with instructions to control its position as well as his head which can be raised and lowered.

The instructions are selected from the menu at the bottom of the screen. There are two modes – either individual instructions or program mode. The idea is to experiment with the individual instructions to get an idea of distance and then to write a program to get Unit to burst all of the balloons in one go.

Use this activity to introduce the principles of computer control.

An excellent introduction to the principles of computer control without having to go to the expense of buying a lot of additional hardware.

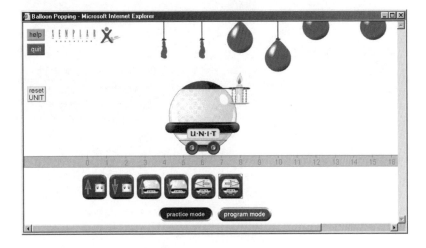

You'll be enthralled with Star Tower if for no other reason than to see just what can be done in a browser. Look out for the random twinkling stars and the owl and the telescope that follow your mouse. Great stuff!

This is a long address so add it to Favourites.

You can access Star Tower at *http://www.apple.com/* but if you want to go directly to the Star Tower site, add *uk/education/ schools/startower/index.html* onto the end of the address.

Toy City

Still on the theme of safe sites, although this time with a commercial bias, Toy City is a superb site for children of all ages, from 4 to 104.

If you can't think what to buy for a present, look no further.

The main purpose of this site is a means of buying toys over the Internet, but it goes much further.

You can search for information about the toys and their suitability for particular children. Toys may be searched for by age, make and type so that parents can be sure they're buying something which is appropriate and that will last more than a couple of weeks.

The toys offered on this site are priced very competitively. Visit Toy City at *http://www.toycity.com/*

Meccano

When Frank Hornby invented Meccano, he launched an engineering system that would retain its popularity for decades.

The clever system of beams, brackets, bolts, nuts and washers continues to maintain its popularity with middle-aged children, but the rise in popularity of plastics has meant that some of the more recent construction products have taken a substantial proportion of Meccano's market.

Don't tread on any of the pieces in your bare feet.

In spite of this, Meccano continues to sell in large quantities and has a loyal following amongst would-be engineers of all ages. Cleverly, Meccano frequently showed pictures of fantastic creations in their advertising campaigns to demonstrate what could be done. Some models would probably require a small mortgage to buy all the parts required to build them.

There is a huge webring for Meccano.

This site puts you in touch with other enthusiasts so you can share ideas and buy or swap parts so that you too can build one of the amazing models.

Of the countless Meccano sites one of my favourites is at *http://www.freenet.edmonton.ab.ca/meccano/*

Teddy bears

If you go down to the woods today, you're sure of a big surprise. If you go to one of their websites, you're in for another surprise. My daughter's eyes lit up when she saw this beautifully presented site from the English Teddy Bear Company. The graphics are superb and the text is easy to access.

Save these sites in your Favourites folder.

The English Teddy Bear Company is at *http://www.teddy. co.uk/*

Some other bear-related sites are:

Teddy Bear UK — *http://www.teddy-bear-uk. com/*

Peter Rabbit and Friends — *http://www.wwwebguides. com/companies/shops/retail/ peter.html*

Bear Faced Cheek — *http://www. bearfacedcheek.freeserve.co.uk/*

Paddington Bear

The marmalade-eating bear found on a railway station in London is currently the most popular bear. (Doubtless this estimate is based on the revenue he generates.)

Your fingers will be sticky after eating marmalade sandwiches. Wash them before using the computer.

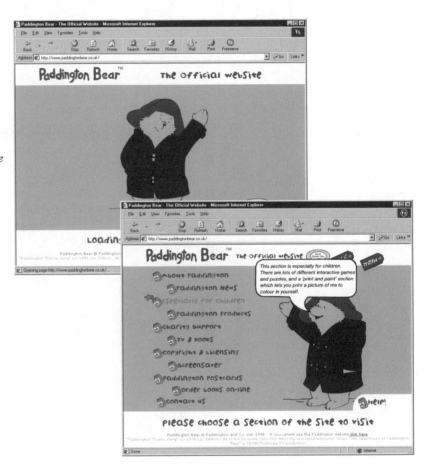

Paddington is a firm favourite with children and the official Paddington Bear website is also a very popular.

The site includes a section about Paddington, where you can learn all about him, and a news section.

Most children will gravitate towards the third section – a series of interactive and educational activities which they will enjoy using.

Under 5's should try *http://www.paddingtonbear.co.uk/*

Lego

When I was 8, I wanted a garage for Christmas. What Father Christmas bought me was one of the first Lego sets – an Esso Garage which I built so many times, I could do it by heart. I could probably still do it today!

Like many kids who are given Lego, more and more bits were added until I had a fair size town. When my children were old enough, we bought them Lego and we all still play with it.

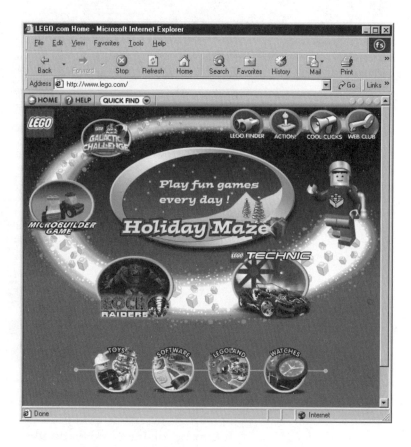

Adults could get hooked on this site too.

The Lego website is a model of good Web design and includes some really clever animations. It gives all the information, history and help you'll need. For example, did you know there are over 80 billion Lego bricks in the world today? I wonder who counted them all!

In addition to information about the actual building bricks, there is also a section about the theme parks and software. Lego currently has seven software titles including some which run on a games console.

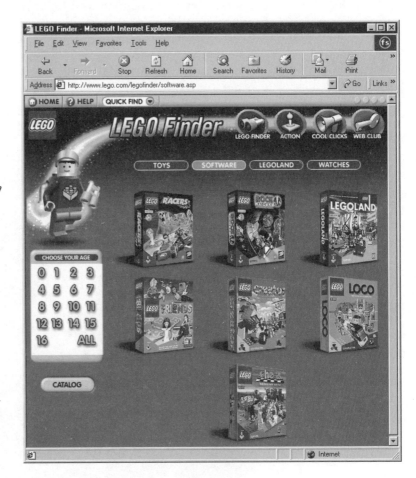

The computer control software adds a whole new dimension to Lego.

The computer games are very addictive.

The main Lego site is at *http://www.lego.com/* but there is also a link to Legoland Windsor at *http://www.lego.com/legoland/windsor/default.asp*.

Fibblesnork Lego Fan Page is also worth visiting at *http://www.lugnet.com/*

Model cars

Scalextric

Slot car racing started in the mid 1950's and reached its height of popularity in the 1960's. At that time there were countless manufacturers of slot car sets for the home. Today, very few remain and Scalextric is probably the largest.

The website details the models and sets and even offers limited edition cars that cannot be purchased anywhere other than on the Scalextric website.

There are lots of electronic gadgets to make it even more fun.

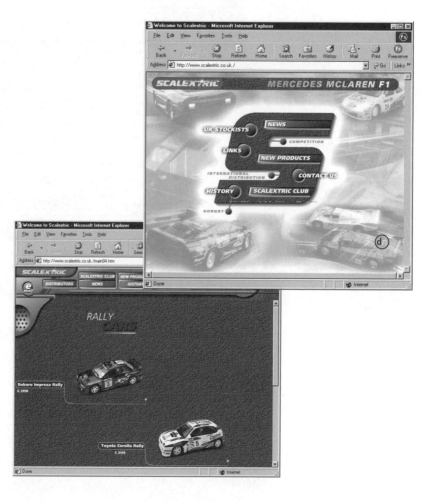

Scalextric is at *http://www.scalextric.co.uk*

Collectables

Slot car racing was born in America where it is still very popular. Apart from Scalextric which is to a scale of 1:32, the format that has survived and flourished is 1:64 – referred to as HO although strictly HO is a little smaller. At half the size, you can get twice as much into the space.

Although the major manufacturers have all but ceased production, there are still several small companies that deal in these models and even manufacture replacement parts for them.

Visit this site for information about starting, building or renovating a collection.

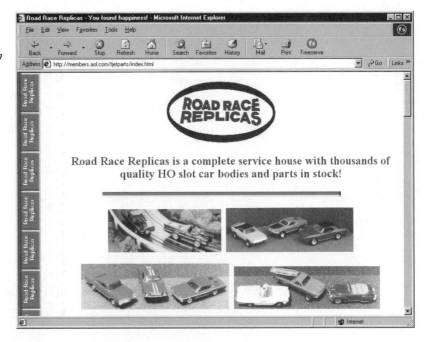

Road Race Replicas have taken it one step further by manufacturing complete models to the very highest standard. Their website shows examples of many of their models which include an amazing amount of detail – remember these models are only about 6cm long.

Road Race Replicas is at *http://members.aol.com/tjetparts/ index.html*

Model railways

Hornby

Apparently, when I was born and my father told his brother that he had a nephew, his response was, "Oh good, we can buy him a train set!"

Five years on, I got my train set, but didn't get much of a look in for some time. When my son was born, it was a similar story but regrettably the pull of computers, Star Wars and other modern pastimes meant that railways didn't get a look in. I suppose it's largely because, having never seen a steam engine in service on a regular basis, having a model of one did not really appeal to him.

If the bug bites, a train set can take up an enormous amount of space.

Hornby is still going strong and exports its models all over the world. It has a constantly changing catalogue of steam, diesel and electric trains with a large selection of rolling stock and track.

Their website is rather like an extension to their catalogue, with copious pictures of engines, carriages and goods wagons. There is a news page and a very interesting section outlining the history of the company.

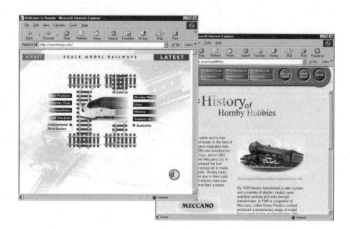

Rather cleverly, the page links are built into an overhead signal gantry.

Hornby is at *http://www.hornby.com/* and *http://www.hornby.co.uk/*

Marklin

If you fancy building a really good model railway but haven't got the space, then the German manufacturer Marklin may have the answer – they produce the smallest scale model railway.

If you're short of space, this could be the answer.

Z Gauge is 1:220 which means you get miles and miles of track in a very small space indeed. Examples have included working models on coffee tables and even in brief cases. One famous model was built in a violin case! Of course this degree of miniaturisation comes at a price.

Marklin, who also produce large scale model railways for use in the garden, are at *http://www.marklin.com/*

More railways

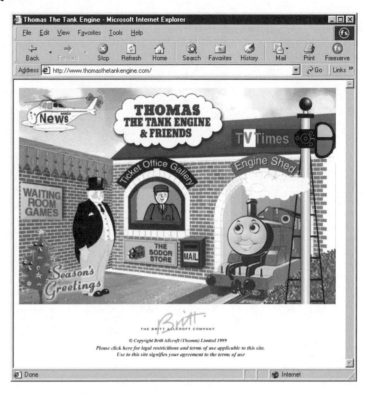

All of the main characters from the original books are here.

The Rev. W Awdry's books about a group of miscellaneous railway engines were a part of my growing up, as they were with many boys who grew up in England in the late 1950's. I remember very well the small landscape books that would fit into a pocket. I also remember being read to by my parents and then reading all of the books again and again. I suppose it was from the Railway Engine series that I learnt to read.

By the time the 1970's had arrived, steam trains had all but vanished from our railways and the Railway Engines books lost much of their appeal to the next generation. That was until Britt Alcroft resurrected the stories and made short TV programmes using a model railway and the voice of Ringo Starr to narrate the stories.

For my generation, this has added appeal – steam trains, model railways and an ex-Beatle in one package.

*Look out for
the mail box to
send email.*

Thomas the Tank Engine & Friends became hugely
successful. Fortunately for
me, my first son was born
at about that time so I had
a ready-made excuse to
buy the videos. Not that I
needed much of an excuse
– Steven loved the stories
as much as I did when I
was his age.

The website captures the
magic of the stories and of
the TV programmes.

You can visit the engine
sheds, meet the engines
and download some
activities like the computer version of join-up-the-dots,
another favourite pastime of days gone by.

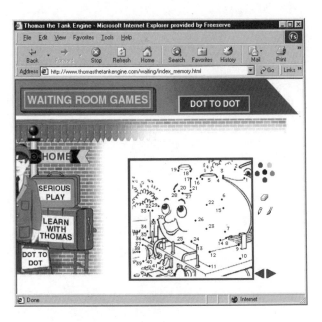

You can visit the home of the railway engines at *http://
www.thomasthetankengine.com/*

Dolls

I think it must be something built into our genes – without doubt we are an acquisitive species. And don't the marketing men know it.

This is marketing aimed directly at kids.

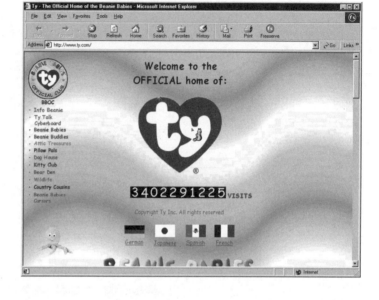

If kids have this collection, this site is an excellent way to introduce them to the Internet.

One of the latest collections is the *ty* series featuring dogs, cats, dolls, bears and various other odds and ends. The collection has caught the imagination of kids in a big way and the backup provided by the website is equally popular. Just look at the hit counter!

The site is in fact a comprehensive database of the collection which is regularly updated with the latest news as to the status of the individuals. Apparently, after a particular individual has been in production for a given period of time, it is 'retired' (discontinued, in old parlance). This adds to the value.

You can visit the ty collection at *http://www.ty.com/*

Barbie

Any website designed for children but offering advice for parents gets my vote. The famous doll that most girls seem to own has her own website laid out, appropriately, in candy colours.

Read the section for adults.

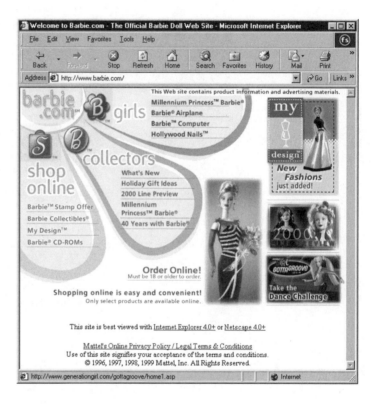

The part that caught my eye was the advice for parents about when to allow their children to use the Web. The advice seems sound and is worth reading, even if you don't read anything else on this site.

The Barbie Doll site does contain an online catalogue where you can view Barbie's wardrobe, but there are also safety tips, registration and a section entitled 'Enjoying barbie.com' which gives some useful advice about using the site.

Barbie Doll is at *http://www.barbie.com/*

Nelvana

Although there is a section for adults, Nelvana is a sort of electronic comic for kids. It's packed full of interactive games and activities for the under 10s, although I have to confess to finding some of them very addictive, (and I'm not under 10).

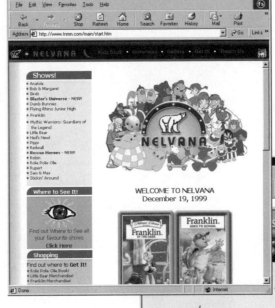

Why buy games when you can get them free?

There is also a section on Rupert the Bear.

The activities include memory games and some very clever painting-by-number pictures, based on some of the Nelvana characters.

During those long school holidays, try logging on to Nelvana at *http://www.tnmn.com/*

Reading

The Children's Bookshop

Children should be encouraged to read and this site will help as it contains details of most children's books. Carefully divided into reading ages, books can be searched by author or title. The files are in text format and can be searched offline.

When you've found what you're looking for, you can place an order there and then.

Children can enjoy books but often need encouragement.

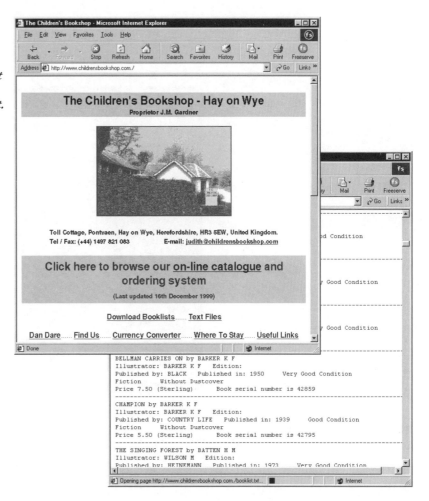

The Children's Bookshop is at *http://www. childrensbookshop.com/*

Technology for girls

GirlTech

The trouble with technology in general, and computers in particular, is that it is male-dominated. From the very first time microcomputers arrived in shops like WH Smith in the early 1980's, you would see the place infested with boys. Only once did I see a girl there and she was being well and truly elbowed to the back.

It's a great shame the Internet isn't encouraging more girls. I'm sure they would find it enjoyable and rewarding, if they were given the opportunity to get involved without boys breathing down their necks telling them how it should be done.

There is a link to a boys' site, but this is really for the girls.

GirlTech is not just about computers; it's about technology and getting girls interested in technology. There are lots of interesting topics and activities which girls should find stimulating.

Come on girls, take a look at Girl Tech at *http://www.girltech.com/*

On a serious note

BritKid

This site is quite unlike any other. It's intended to make kids think about the world around them. It confronts racism and racial issues in a way in which they can understand. There are situations to resolve and descriptions to get you thinking.

This site is well worth visiting, and not just by children.

Try to spend time with your child going through this site.

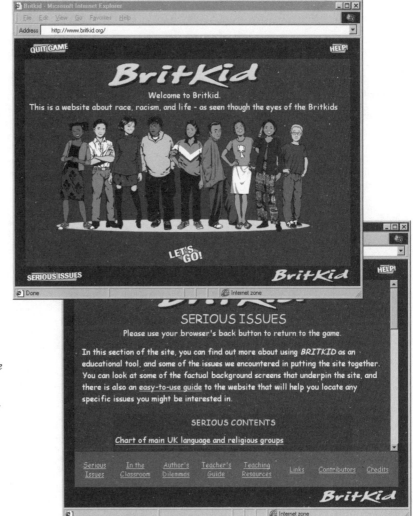

Schools would do well to include this site as part of a personal development programme of study.

Britkid is at *http://www.britkid.org/*

Other kids' sites

Beakman

Beakman at *http://www.beakman.com/* includes links to the library of photos taken by the Hubble Space Telescope. There are also pictures of the other planets in our solar system.

Scrabble

The official Scrabble site at *http://www.scrabble.com/* is really for adults, but older children will get a lot from it.

Some of these sites are really for adults, but teenagers will usually be able to get something from them.

Toy Town

Visit Toy Town at *http://www.toytown.co.uk/* to get a rundown of the latest and greatest toys.

Yahooligans

Yahooligans is a site specially for kids with all sorts of activities kids love. For safe fun visit *http://www. yahooligans.com/*

Your Gross Body

This site claims to be the yuckiest on the Internet. Topics include poop, gas, zits, sweat, ear wax and dandruff. Your Gross Body is at *http://www.yucky.com/body*

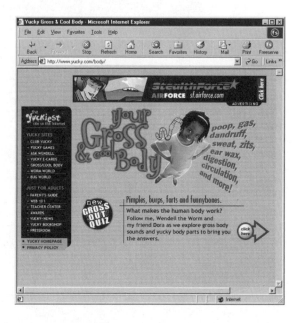

Education

All of the World Wide Web could be regarded as educational. Here, though, are some sites which stand out from the rest as being of particular use for research.

Covers

Chapter Eighteen

The Arthur C Clarke Foundation

History will show that there have been many visionaries of the 20th Century, but none more prominent than Arthur C Clarke.

This site is packed with fascinating information.

His thinking was years ahead of its time. He invented the communication satellite during the 1940s when the world was at war and we were flying around in propeller driven aeroplanes. At the time, people must have thought his idea was, to say the very least, irrelevant. Today the communication satellite is as much a part of our lives as the telephone. Indeed, much of our transcontinental communications rely very heavily on his work.

Now in retreat in Sri Lanka, Arthur C Clarke is probably most famous as the author of 2001 and as a television personality pondering the mysteries of Earth and beyond.

His website gives a fascinating insight into the man and his work, with links for education.

The Arthur C Clarke Foundation website is at *http://www.acclarke.co.uk/*

Why?

I was bought up to continually ask, "Why?" Both the natural world and our modern technological world are full of wondrous creations. But so much of what is around us is just taken for granted. Nobody seems interested in understanding anything. We just use it and accept it without so much as a passing thought.

This site provides lots of answers.

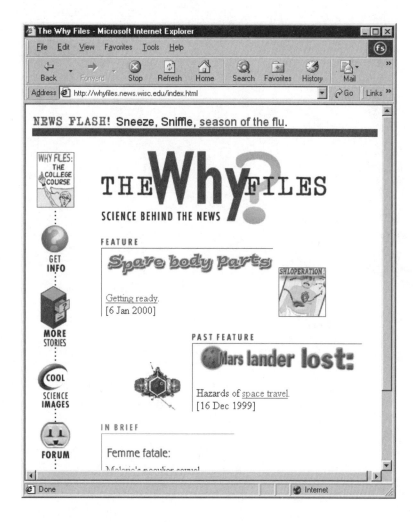

The Why? Files site delivers the science behind the news. Regularly updated with new stories, this website is well worth visiting. The Why? Files site is at *http://whyfiles. news.wisc.edu/index.html*

Roundo

If knowledge is power then Roundo must be one of the most powerful sites on the Web as it provides links to some of the best of the Web's educational sites.

This site will point you to some of the best educational websites.

Although aimed primarily at UK education, this site provides pointers to material which is relevant to all seekers of knowledge, wherever they may reside.

It is thoughtfully divided into subjects and clicking on one of the subjects provides a page of links to quality websites, many with a description of the site content.

The sites have been carefully selected and categorised so you can be sure that you get what you want, and what you get is worth having. Visitors are requested to submit quality websites to add to the list of links ensuring the site is as up to date as possible. Roundo is at *http://www. roundo.net/*

Discovery

When I first had a satellite dish, I found that most of the free channels were free for one simple reason: what was being offered wasn't worth paying for. One notable exception was (and still is) the Discovery Channel.

This is an excellent site to back up the programs on the Discovery TV Channel.

The main features of this site are a mixture of news stories of scientific interest and articles to support forthcoming programmes. These are supported with web cams and merchandising offers.

Discovery Online is frequently updated with lots of current stories liberally illustrated with some superb pictures. To find out more, visit *http://www.discovery. com/*

Booksearch

Books provide a great deal of pleasure for people of all ages. There is a huge amount of information on the Web about all sort of books.

To find the exact book you want, go to *http://www. nwnet.co.uk/BFG* – the home page of Bookfinder General. There is a very friendly search facility that will help you locate your book.

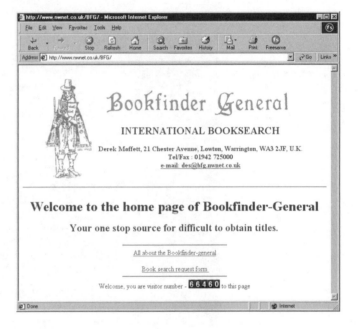

New York Times Books	—	*http://www.nytimes.com/books*
Computer Step	—	*http://www.computerstep.com/*
Questions Publishing	—	*http://www.questpub.co.uk/*
Blackwell's	—	*http://bookshop.blackwell.co.uk/*
Waterstones	—	*http://www.waterstones.co.uk/*

This is only a small sample of related websites.

Books

Searching for books can be a little tiresome but this site can help. It has links into several major distributors with online ordering. Choosing and buying books has never been simpler.

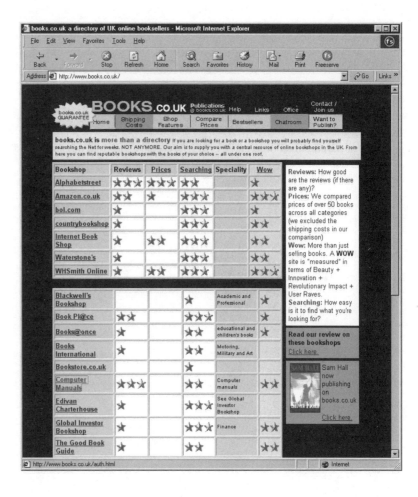

Use this site to locate book retailers.

The site lists all of the major online book sellers and provides a guide as to the service they provide. The star-rating system indicates the quality of service provided. In particular, they consider if reviews of books are provided (including the quality of the reviews) and the price of the books offered.

Books can be found at *http://www.books.co.uk/*

Encyclopedia Britannica

Probably the best known encyclopedia in the world is also online. To support their books and their CD ROMs, EB have this website which contains a mine of fascinating information.

The information in books can go out of date. Information on the Web can be updated.

The Encyclopedia Britannica website regularly hosts major features on a wide variety of topics, often ones which are in the headlines. The text is clear and easily accessible, and liberally dotted with links to other related information.

To be able to use this site you need to subscribe and there are special deals for families and students.

This is a truly excellent site and can be found at *http://www.eb.com/*

A spin-off from this is Britannica at *http://www.britannica.com/* which lists useful websites.

The Book of Clichés

Use the Favourites facility in your browser to avoid having to repeatedly type long Web addresses.

Just to underline the diversity of the Internet, we have clichés. Personally, I avoid clichés like the plague. A cliché to me is like a red rag to a bull. In fact, I go to the ends of the earth to avoid clichés. If you are of a different leaning, then this site will provide you with lots of 'off-the-cuff' clichés to amaze your friends and confound your enemies.

The address is rather long, but worth entering. It's *http:// utopia.knoware.nl/users/sybev/cliche/index.htm*

Web elements

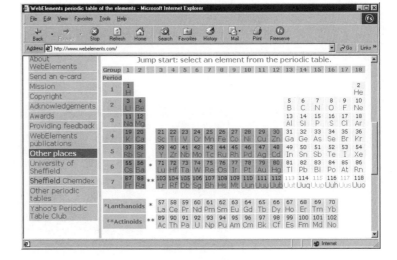

This site contains just about every piece of information, including non-scientific, about all of the elements.

I've always been fascinated with the periodic table of elements. The layout and its evolution have been a constant source of wonder to me. As have the contents. For those studying Chemistry, this site is a mine of information.

Superbly presented, this site gives all the important information about each of the elements. Simply click on an element in the table and you're presented with all the details about its molecular make-up as well as some interesting bits like who discovered it. Point to *http://www.webelements.com/*

Other educational sites

Alphabet Street

Alphabet Street is an online bookseller which frequently has some very attractive special offers on selected books. Visit Alphabet Street at *http://www.alphabetstreet.com/*

Chemistry

For Chemistry fans, this antipodean website has some very useful material including some tests and quizzes. Visit *http://www.chemistry.co.nz/chem.htm*

The Chemist's Art Gallery at *http://www.csc.fi/lul/chem/graphics.html* features some amazing pictures and animations of chemical reactions.

These are just some of the excellent education sites to visit.

Fractals

Fractals are computer-generated pictures of enormous complexity. To find out more about them, visit *http://web.pinknet.cz/fractal/* but beware, some of the screens take a long time to download. But they're worth the wait.

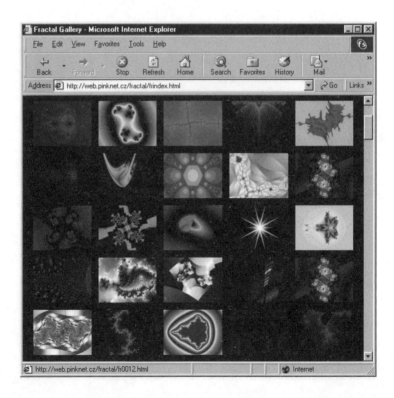

Geography

National Geographic is probably the most widely known publication of its type. The online version at *http://www.nationalgeographic.com/* will not disappoint. High quality pictures and maps accompany very readable articles on a wide range of topics from the natural world.

 The ~ symbol is called a tilde and can be found next to the Return key.

History

Essential reading for all History students is History Net. Whether it is wars, navigation or personality profiles, it's sure to be here. Point to *http://www.thehistorynet.com/*

The European Royal History website contains biographies of many of the European Royals down the ages. Lots of well written text, supported by appropriate pictures. European Royal History is at *http://www.eurohistory.com/*

History Search provides a 'limited area search of the Ancient and Medieval Internet' at *http://argos.evansville.edu/* (There are also links to some ancient sites.)

History Today Magazine is now online at *http://www.historytoday.com/*

Like the paper magazine, the online version is filled with quality copy on a diverse range of topics from 'Why Hess flew to Britain' to 'Portrait of Britain AD1'. Also featured are links to other sites, a powerful search facility and guidelines should you wish to contribute.

Mathematics

The Maths Website is maintained by the Oundle School in the UK and provides links to some of the best maths related websites from around the world. To find out more visit *http://www.argonet.co.uk/oundlesch/mlink.html*

Anyone who thinks maths is boring hasn't visited Mathsnet. This site is packed with interactive activities, animations, articles and software. Point to *http://www.anglia.co.uk/education/mathsnet*

Another great mathematics site – Megamaths – is sure to

capture the imagination of the young and not so young. Megamaths can be found at *http://www.c3.lanl.gov/mega-math/*

The New Scientist Magazine

The New Scientist Magazine is now online. Apart from some excellent editorial, there is also a jobs section and your chance to voice your opinion. Point to *http://www.newscientist.com/*

Tomorrow's World

Although some of these sites are primarily intended for a particular country, the content of most is relevant for any English speaking user.

Tomorrow's World is one of the longest running programmes on UK television. The website at *http://www.bbc.co.uk/tw* contains material to support the programme. It also features some of the latest stories from the world of science and technology.

The Perseus Project

The Perseus Project is an 'evolving digital library of resources for the study of the ancient world' and may be found at *http://www.perseus.tufts.edu/*

Poetry Daily

Poetry Daily provides exactly what it says at *http://www.poems.com/*

Prehistoric Sites

Prehistoric Sites is a guide to the ancient monuments around the United Kingdom. Find out more at *http://www.henge.demon.co.uk/*

Religious Education Resource Centre

Although this is billed as the Religious Education Resource Centre for the UK, its content is just as relevant in other parts of the world. Point to *http://www.ajbird.demon.co.uk/*

Volcanos

Surfing the Net with kids? Volcanos is at *http://www.surfnetkids.com/volcano.htm*. Provides everything you ever wanted to know about volcanoes. Try also *http://volcano.und.nodak.edu/vw.html*

News and information

People need to keep up to date with world and local events for a variety of different reasons, but it's not always easy to catch the latest news. The morning paper doesn't get delivered, your train is late so you miss the evening broadcast and all of a sudden you're behind the times. The Internet can help to keep you informed.

Covers

Chapter Nineteen

Newspapers

The Washington Post

Virtually all of the world's national newspapers and many provincial newspapers have a website. They are clearly very successful and widely used which is surprising as I observe that, in general, people still seem to prefer to read paper rather than screens. But, they are free.

The Washington Post is typical of these sites, being effectively an electronic version of the paper that comes through the letter box each morning.

Online newspapers aren't always as convenient as their traditional counterparts.

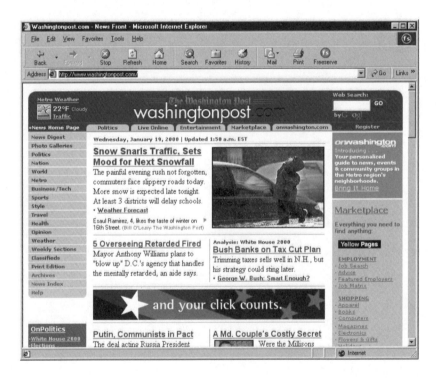

It has the usual mix of news, opinion and sport, together with interviews and articles of general interest.

What the electronic version offers that the hardcopy version doesn't is a search facility so that you can search for a specific story or article.

The online Washington Post is at *http://www. washingtonpost.com/*

The Mirror

The UK's Daily Mirror website is similar to the paper, being less 'heavy' and containing some interesting features such as a crossword puzzle. The Mirror Online is at *http://www.mirror.co.uk/*

Worldwide News

A list of over 500 of the world's online papers can be found at *http://www.onlinenewspapers.com/* or *http://www.webwombat.com.au/*

If you don't want to go trawling through this pile of virtual papers, then try...

The Australian (Au)	—	*http://www.theaustralian.com.au/*
The Daily Courier (Ca)	—	*http://www.ok.bc.ca/dc/*
Jewish Chronicle (UK)	—	*http://www.jchron.co.uk/*
Evening Post (NZ)	—	*http://www.evpost.co.nz/*
The Times (UK)	—	*http://www.the-times.co.uk/*

BBC News

The BBC are world famous for their efficient and unbiased delivery of news into our living rooms. The trouble is, if you don't happen to be at home at the right times, you won't get to hear what is happening.

Unlike TV news, you can view Web news whenever you want.

For those who haven't got a fast modem, there is a link to a text only version.

BBC Online News enables you to keep abreast of world developments at a time which suits yourself and not the programme planners.

The site is divided into categories so you can easily select the item you want, but if you prefer there is a search facility which will track down a specific item for you.

BBC News is at *http://news.bbc.co.uk/*

Teletext

Many modern television sets are equipped to receive text which is simultaneously broadcast with the normal television signal. The 'pages' contain a variety of news and information but are limited by relatively low resolution resulting in a lack of detail both in story content and graphic display.

These provide a great deal more detail than teletext on a TV.

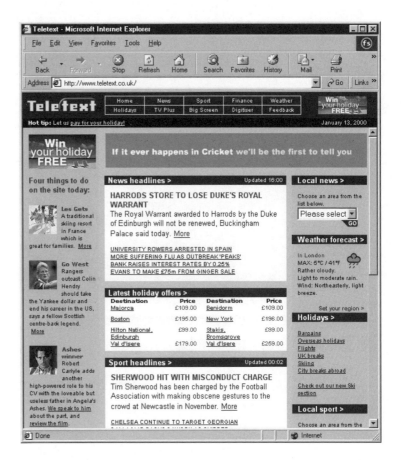

Teletext on the Internet contains a lot more information than the TV version and is a good source for news, travel and television times. Teletext on the Internet is at *http://www.teletext.com/*

For details about the latest video games, including the Top Ten of the moment, visit *http://www.teletext.com/digitiser/*

Independent Radio News

Radio listeners will be familiar with Independent Radio News broadcasts. These hourly updates are also available on the Web and take a similar format to the broadcast news: all the headlines first and then the details.

The website opens with the headlines and a brief outline of the story. Clicking on the headline will take you to a page where there is a more detailed account.

This news is updated every hour.

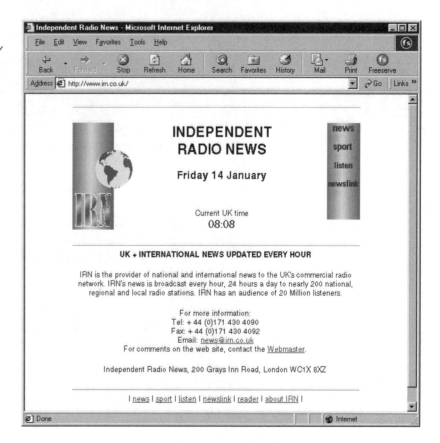

Independent Radio News is at *http://www.irn.co.uk/*

What's New

What's New contains travel information and a booking facility. There are some very useful links to other sites. Visit *http://www.whatsnew.com/msie/intro/*

Weather

World weather

In some parts of the world, a conversation without reference to the weather is almost unheard of. Phrases like 'miserable morning', 'should stay nice' and 'blowing up a bit' trip off the tongue almost daily. For many, the changing state of the weather is nothing short of a preoccupation, whilst others – like farmers and fishermen – depend on it for their livelihood.

Check out this site before going on a skiing holiday.

Whether they are more reliable than other means of ascertaining whether to take a brolly or not, I'll leave others to decide. All I'll add is that last winter I shovelled 3 inches of 'damp and slightly overcast' off my drive!

You can get local weather forecasts for any part of the country.

These are just a few of the weather related websites.

CNN Weather at *http://www.cnn.com/weather/cities/world.html* provides weather information for every region of the planet. Simply choose your location and click the Go button to get up-to-the-minute information.

Weather Post

Weather Post at *http://www.weatherpost.com/* offers a good service. Of special note is the ice/snow forecast for skiers.

Genealogy

If you've ever wondered about your forefathers, you could find the answers on the Internet. Genealogy is becoming a very popular Internet specialism with several sites offering you the chance to find out more about your past.

Of them all, RootsWeb at *http://www.rootsweb.com/* is a good starting point largely because it offers a superb on-screen tutorial on the subject of genealogy. The tutorial is broken down into a series of lessons taking you from the very basic principles to advanced searching techniques.

The tutorials use lots of graphics and will take some time to download.

Genealogy is sure to reveal any skeletons in the wardrobe.

Family Search is also worth investigating at *http://www. familysearch.org/*

The Public Record Office

For many, the thought of researching public records will be seen as a sure cure for insomnia. How wrong you are. This is a fascinating subject brought to life by the website of the Public Record Office.

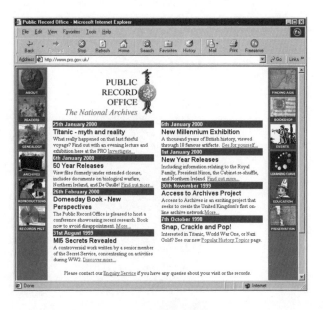

This is a fascinating topic which could reveal some surprises about your past.

This site is very well thought out with links to topical stories which are backed by PRO documentation. Forthcoming features and events are also well sign-posted.

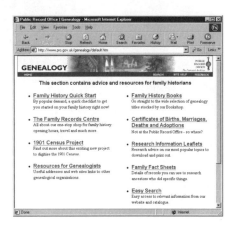

There is also an interesting section for budding genealogists wishing to find out more about their ancestry. This section includes some help screens and some pointers to get you started delving into the archives.

The PRO is at *http://www.pro.gov.uk/*

The RAC

The website for the Royal Automobile Club is a site well worth visiting before any car journey beyond the local shops. First, it is updated every 30 minutes so you can be sure the information is recent and relevant. Second, it has some features which will make driving a lot more pleasurable and consequently safer.

Check out this site before going on a car journey.

The section headed Live Traffic News is just that: live information about news in your immediate area. After you choose the area you are currently in, the information is quickly returned about accidents, road works or any other hold ups.

If you're touring the UK, this site is essential as it provides a list of good hotels, bed & breakfast and guest house accommodation.

Naturally there are links to other RAC services like their breakdown recovery service, which is still the backbone of the organisation's work.

Careful planning is vital for a safe journey. It's never a good idea to just point your car in about the right direction and hope that you can work it out as you go.

The RAC Route Planner, which now extends to most of Europe, requires you to enter your starting location and your destination, which can be names of towns or just postcodes. You also have the opportunity of entering a location to travel through (perhaps for a stopover), and the choice of whether you want the fastest route or the shortest. When that information has been entered, type in your email address and press the 'Submit' button.

You'll be emailed your route from door to door taking into account local road and traffic conditions.

The RAC is at *http://www.rac.co.uk/*

The RAC's biggest rival is the AA, and their website is at *http://www.theaa.com/*

Worldwide Traffic Congestion

For worldwide news of the state of the roads, log on to *http://www.internettrafficreport.com/,* the address of the Internet Traffic Report website.

If you have a laptop computer and the facility to access the Internet on the move, refer to this site frequently.

For women...

Handbag.com

The general consensus seems to be that women are not well represented on the Web, yet they are potentially the largest 'untapped' market.

Recognising this shortcoming, several sites have sprung up which are designed specifically to meet the needs of women.

Amid a blaze of publicity, *http://www.handbag.com/* was launched as a magazine for women, by women. The site features a combination of news, views and articles with a distinctly feminine approach.

In addition to merely visiting the site, you can get the Handbag CD ROM which includes a copy of Internet Explorer. The disc is thoughtfully wrapped in a case looking like a handbag and coloured in a choice of four nail-polish colours.

You can get free email through this site.

The format is similar to many magazines aimed at women – there are features about shopping, health and beauty and home and garden. But this magazine also includes features like live polls and up-to-date financial advice.

Although aimed at women, there is a lot of useful information for everyone.

Icircle
http://www.icircle.com/ is very similar to handbag.com in so far as it's pitched at the same audience.

Women drivers
http://www.womanmotorist.com/ is specifically for women motorists, who seem to get a better deal than men from insurance companies. That should stop a few jokes!

Make-up
Health and beauty seem to be never far away from female websites and *http://www.changeslive.com/* could help with the beauty part as it provides guidance on buying and using make-up.

Other news sites

News Page	—	*http://www.newspage.com/*
NewsBytes News Network	—	*http://www.nbnn.com/*
Reuters	—	*http://www.reuters.com/*
Sunday Times	—	*http://www.sunday-times.co.uk/*
Financial Times	—	*http://www.ft.com/*
The Press Association	—	*http://www.pa.press.net/*
The Sporting Life	—	*http://www.sporting-life.com/*
This is London	—	*http://www.thisislondon.co.uk/*
Anorak	—	*http://www.anorak.co.uk/*
FutureNet	—	*http://www.futurenet.com/*
Newspaper Society	—	*http://www.newspapersoc.org. uk/*
The Church Times	—	*http://www.churchtimes.co.uk/*
Times Educational Supplement	—	*http://www.tes.co.uk/*
Media UK	—	*http://www.mediauk.com/ directory*
The PRnet Newswire	—	*http://www.prnet.co.uk/*

Other information sites

Skeptics Society	—	*http://www.skeptic.com/*
HM Treasury	—	*http://www.hm-treasury.gov. uk/*
UK Weather	—	*http://www.meto.govt.uk/*
BBC Weather Centre	—	*http://www.bbc.co.uk/weather*
Dept of Meteorology	—	*http://www.met.rdg.ac.uk/ ~brugge*

Organisations

This section includes details of mainly environmental and humanitarian organisations, although there are also some others.

Covers

Chapter Twenty

UNICEF

The United Nations International Children's Emergency Fund needs little introduction. The UNICEF website outlines many of the organisation's current projects throughout the world in simple, easily accessible language.

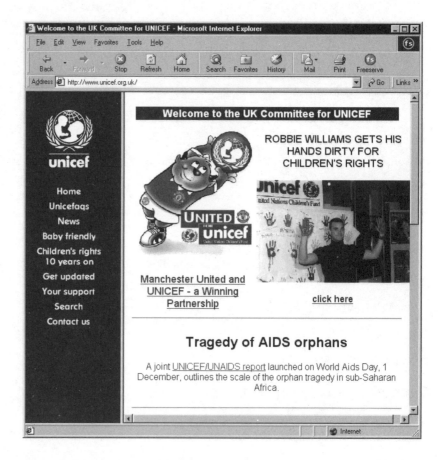

This site provides information about current issues, like the tragedy of the AIDS orphans. There is also a section showing how you can help this organisation.

UNICEF is at *http://www.unicef.org.uk/*

Help the Aged

It's a sad but true fact that over one third of our senior citizens live alone. These are the people who have worked hard all their lives, even fought for our country, and yet have to struggle to keep warm.

Help the Aged is at *http://www.helptheaged.org.uk/*

One World

This site has links to other humanitarian sites.

One World is an appropriate title for this site which looks at a variety of humanitarian issues from around the world. Apart from its own pages, there are links to most of the humanitarian organisations.

One World is at *http://www.oneworld.org/*

Greenpeace

We didn't inherit the earth from our parents, we are minding it for our children. The earth has paid a huge price for 20th Century technology: we take from the Earth and then spew back the waste with little regard for the long or short term consequences.

Greenpeace brings the world's attention to what we are doing to our planet. Its website outlines many of the key issues.

Earth is the only home we have and it's got to last a long time.

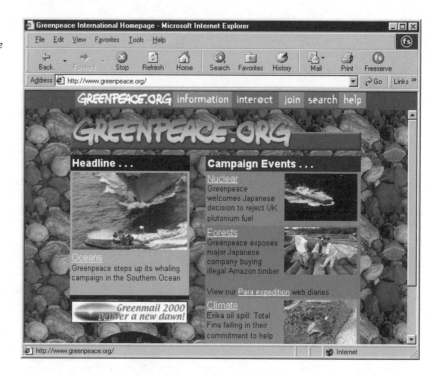

Greenpeace is at *http://www.greenpeace.org/*

Friends of the Earth

Like Greenpeace, Friends of the Earth are concerned with environmental issues. Their website also outlines some of the major environmental problems.

Friends of the Earth is at *http://www.foe.co.uk/*

Amnesty International

Not all countries have a justice system based on a fair trial. As a result there are countless people throughout the world who have been imprisoned for political reasons and many are living in appalling conditions.

Amnesty International speaks out for all people who are oppressed for whatever reason.

 This is a good site for discussion groups at school.

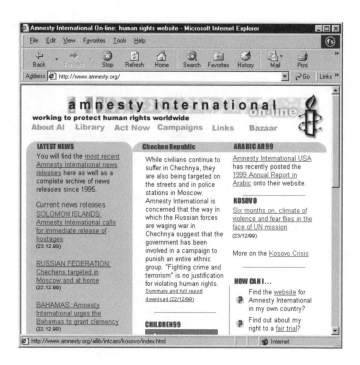

The site contains a great deal of information about Amnesty International, including details of current campaigns of which, tragically, there are many.

As can be seen from the illustration, the site is updated daily with news about current issues from around the world.

The Library section details past campaigns that Amnesty International has worked on, and also gives a list of other humanitarian organisations with hotlinks to take you straight to their sites.

Amnesty International is at *http://www.amnesty.org/*

The Samaritans

Modern living certainly does not suit everyone. For some, it's all too much and, for one reason or another, the situation appears irresolvable. Desperation then takes over, sometimes with tragic consequences.

Help is at hand from probably the best known counselling organisation in the world: the Samaritans.

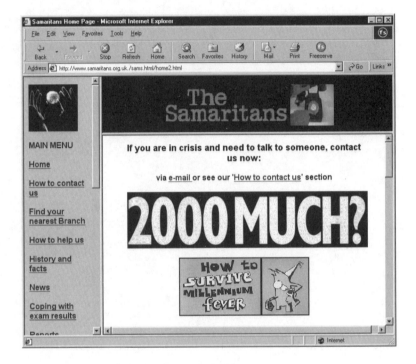

It is now possible to email the Samaritans as well as telephone for confidential counselling. There are many centres across the country and they are all included here for those who might wish to contact them in the traditional manner, rather than electronically. Full contact details are provided.

Their website also includes current news about the Samaritans and some practical advice about how you can help.

The Samaritans site is *http://www.samaritans.org.uk/*

Christian Aid

Christian Aid is one of the best known charities in the world. Its work in war-torn areas and scenes of natural disaster is well known to all of us.

The Christian Aid website brings some of the good work to our homes, including a selection of links to other sites.

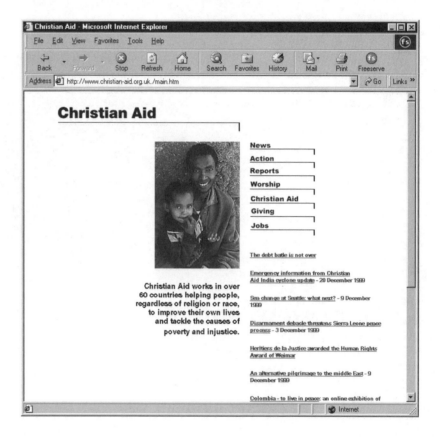

Whatever your religious persuasion, it seems to me that organisations such as Christian Aid should be supported to enable them to bring relief to the suffering of millions throughout the world.

Christian Aid helps all people, regardless of their religion. It may be contacted at *http://www.christian-aid.org.uk/*

Save the Children

Another great humanitarian organisation that does so much good throughout the world. Save The Children also has an excellent website which contains a great deal of information about the plight of children throughout the world.

Its website is at *http://www.savethechildren.org.uk/* although it may also be accessed via the One World website at *http://www.oneworld.org/*

This is another great website for use in schools.

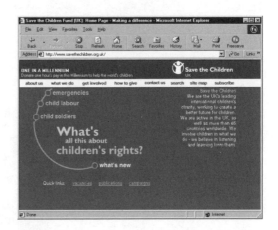

Other organisations

Government Information	—	*http://www.open.gov.uk/*
New Deal	—	*http://www.newdeal.gov.uk/*
RSPCA Online	—	*http://www.rspca.org.uk/*
Inst. for Global Comms	—	*http://www.igc.org/*
New Internationalist	—	*http://oneworld.org/ni/ index.html*
Cyber Law Centre	—	*http://www.cyberlawcentre. org.uk/*
Oxfam	—	*http://www.oxfam.org.uk/*

Technology

What materialistic people we are! This chapter is devoted to some of the technology we have surrounded ourselves with.

Covers

Chapter Twenty-One

Motor cars

Apart from a house, a motor car is likely to be the single most expensive purchase made by a family.

Just before my 17th birthday, my father (who was a very keen driver) told me, "If you choose to learn to drive, you'll have your hand in your pocket for evermore". How true that was. But the promise of increased personal mobility, and the pull of the freedom that that provided, were too great. On my 17th birthday I started driving lessons and, 5 months later, I passed my test. Twenty-odd years later, I still haven't stopped spending.

Oil is running out. Fast.

Financial implications aside, the motor car has a great deal to answer for in terms of pollution, global warming and deaths due to road traffic accidents. Not to mention the rape of the natural environment to provide roads to carry an ever-increasing army of horseless carriages up and down the country. Look at the statistics at *http://doric.bart.ucl.ac.uk/web/ben/*

In the 100 years since the first motor car clattered along a cobblestoned path at little more than walking pace, we have learnt to rely on them.

Stand on a bridge over any motorway leading into a major city during the two or three hours before the city awakes and you'll see an endless stream of cars, usually occupied by just one person – the driver. At the end of the day, the same stream of traffic is back on the motorway heading in the opposite direction.

The amount of fuel being consumed for this daily two-way trek into town is beyond comprehension. If you must drive to work, and the journey must be alone, then at least use a car which has a little less impact on the proceedings.

Mercedes Benz recently joined forces with stylish Swiss watchmaker Swatch to produce the SMART. This is a tiny compact two seater which just oozes style. Although not strictly speaking 'green', it's 'greener' than most.

The SMART is about the same length as most cars are wide and so it can park at 90° to the kerb which means it occupies less than half the space of other cars.

Its 3-cylinder engine returns over 60 miles to the gallon, yet the low-pressure turbocharger and sequential gears (rather like those used in Formula One racing cars) mean the SMART is quite quick. It also has all the creature comforts normally associated with luxury cars – electric windows, air-conditioning and, optionally, leather upholstery.

Although made in France, the SMART is available in most EEC countries.

Although quite cheap to buy and run, the SMART has some very clever features.

All the body panels are self-coloured plastic and can be changed in about an hour. So, if you decide that you don't want to drive a blue car to work, you can buy a new set of panels in another colour.

The SMART is made under licence in France but there are several importers in most countries.

Start off visiting *http://www.wykehams.com/* and then go on to *http://www.ksb.co.uk/* before looking at *http://www.planetmoto. co.uk/* to see how to change the panels.

Official websites

Virtually every motor manufacturer from around the world has at least one website, known as the official website, and in most cases typing in the make of the car followed by *.com/* will take you there.

Many people latch onto this and visit the exotic sites of *http://www.bmw.com/* or *http://www.porsche.com/*, but don't forget the sites of some of the more ordinary cars like *http://www.renault.com/* or *http://www.honda.com/*

Don't forget some of the more common car makes.

Audi	—	*http://www.audi.com/*
Fiat	—	*http://www.fiat.com/*
McLaren	—	*http://www.mclaren.co.uk/*
MG	—	*http://www.mgcars.com/*
Mini	—	*http://www.mini.com/*
Rover	—	*http://www.rovercars.com/*
Saab	—	*http://www.saab.com/*
Volkswagen	—	*http://www.vw.com/*
Volvo	—	*http://www.volvo.com/*

Unofficial websites

In many ways, these are much more fun. These are the sites built by enthusiasts – 'anoraks', as some people call them. If anyone has a craving for information about a particular car, then the Web is the place to go.

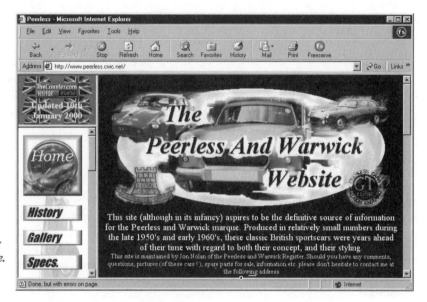

The more obscure the make of car, the more likely it is to be there.

A good stating point is Yahoo's website (*http://www. yahoo.com/*) which lists thousands of sites. First click on Autos (in the Leisure section) and a further thirty-odd categories will be listed. This will lead you to sites from around the world dedicated to a particular make or model of car. The more obscure, the more likely it is to be there, like this site dedicated to a hitherto little-known British car of the 1960's, the Peerless.

Offbeat bits

For collectors of miscellaneous facts, the Rolls Royce facts site at *http://www.darkforce.com/royce/facts.htm* is full of interesting offbeat snippets. Nothing to do with the Rolls Royce company, just an individual who likes 'Rollers'. Or is it 'Royces'?

Also worth a visit is Team.Net at *http://www.team.net/*

Grey or parallel?

Parallel imports

The current cry in the UK is that cars are overpriced compared to other areas of the EEC. This has led to individuals importing cars themselves. This in turn has led to individuals forming companies that specialise in importing cars built to UK standards at significantly less than official dealers charge.

Grey imports

A grey import is a car that has been built for one market but has been bought into another market either as a new or used car. As far as the manufacturers are concerned, these cars do not exist, so warranties may be an issue in the country to which they are being imported.

The cars are usually sourced from rich countries like Japan where they have frequently been saved from the scrap heap after a relatively short life stuck in Tokyo's traffic jams and/or raced round car-parks. They are then sent to poorer countries (like the UK) where they are resold.

Cars built for the Japanese market are not usually rust-proofed to the same degree as European cars.

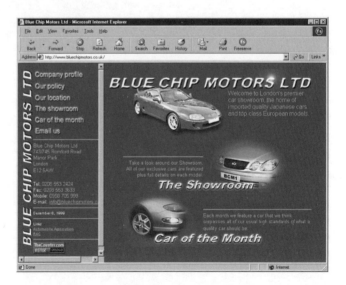

If you want to get a parallel import, try *http://www.wundercars.co.uk/* or *http://www.sussex-imports.co.uk/*. If you're thinking about a grey import, look no further than *http://www.bluechipmotors.co.uk/*

Buying and selling

Second-hand car dealers seem to hold a special place in the hearts of the car-buying public. Survey after survey usually places them somewhere between double-glazing salesmen and estate agents.

But nobody has to use them. You can buy and sell cars yourself, if you don't mind a little bit of hassle.

When selling your car, you'll first need to find out what it's worth. Parkers Guide is as good as any guide and their website is at *http://www.parkers.co.uk/*

When buying or selling a car, it pays to do your homework.

You'll then need to place an advert and Autohunter can help with this. Go to *http://www.autohunter.co.uk/* to compose a really cheap advert, placed for two weeks.

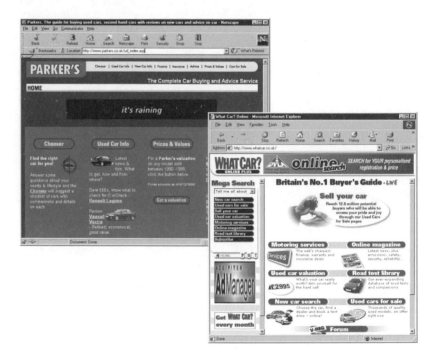

When deciding on which car to buy, visit *http://www.whatcar.co.uk/* to find out about the pros and cons of just about every model from the last 10 years.

Also worth investigating is Autobytel at *http://www.autobytel.co.uk/*

Global Positioning

A few years ago the US Military launched a constellation of satellites which now orbit the Earth. At any time and at any place on Earth, at least three of these satellites will be 'visible'. With the right hardware and software it is possible for anyone to establish their exact position (including altitude) and speed.

This site gives more information about Global Positioning.

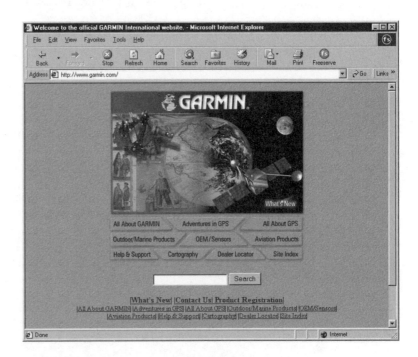

This is the Global Positioning System and Garmin are one of the major manufacturers of GPS receivers. These may be either self-contained handsets about the size of a mobile phone with a keypad and screen, or just a receiver which can be connected to a portable computer. GPS is of limited use in a car in this country as the signposts and maps are more than adequate. But in the air, on water or on a road in another country, this is an excellent method of preventing yourself from becoming lost.

Garmin's website is at *http://www.garmin.com/* where you can find out more about GPS and about Garmin's products.

More and more motor manufacturers are fitting GPS systems to their cars. These so-called SatNavs often include a CD ROM system containing road information to provide a moving map display.

Apart from helping you find your way, GPS is being used in an increasing number of imaginative ways.

BMW recently announced a GPS-based system which points the car's headlamps into corners. Because the car 'knows' where it is, and connects this information with an accurate map, it knows what the road is like immediately in front. It predicts curves in the road and points the headlamps into the curve providing better illumination both into and through the curve. Claimed to transform night driving, the system should be available on production cars by 2002.

GPS has more uses than simply finding your way.

Available now is RAC's Trackstar which uses GPS to track your car if it is stolen. A transmitter is fitted into the car in a location known only to the fitter, and if the car is tampered with it sends out a signal which is tracked. The exact whereabouts of the car can be tracked to within a few feet.

Other benefits are that, in the event of a breakdown, the RAC will know exactly where you are (even which side of the road). A built-in voice link enables the driver to contact the recovery or emergency services at the touch of a button.

For more information on Trackstar, visit *http://www. ractrackstar.co.uk/*

Computers

It would be difficult to write a book such as this without at least a passing reference to websites associated with the computer industry. There are a huge number of sites relating to computers. Some relate to hardware, some to software. Others provide help, or are somewhere in between.

Games consoles

The games console market is huge and the main players are Sega, Nintendo and Sony.

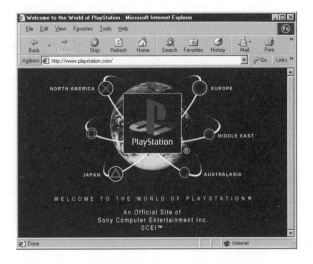

The websites are as slick as the games. The main ones to visit are...

Sega   —   *http://www.sega.com/* and
                          http://www.dreamcast.com/

Nintendo   —   *http://www.nintendo.com/* and
                          http://www.gameboy.com/

Sony   —   *http://www.sony.com/* and
                          http://www.playstation.com/

Networking

Even with only a few computers, it can be worth networking them. Networking has two major benefits. First, the users can share resources – rather than each person having their own printer (all of which would be idle for most of the time) you can provide one really good printer and let everyone share it. The second benefit of networking is that people will be able to access their work from any of the computers on the network.

In the home, even with two computers, there are significant benefits to linking them and it is incredibly cheap and easy to do.

There are some superb multi-user games that can be played across a network of two or more computers.

For more information on networking, see the appropriate title from the 'in easy steps' series table on the inside-back cover of this book.

Netgear offers an assortment of products to enable you to link anything between two and eight computers as a peer-to-peer network – which basically means that each computer shares the resources (hard discs and printers) of any of the others. For backup purposes this is an excellent solution as one computer can use another's backup device.

Netgear also have some interesting ideas on linking telephones.

Netgear are at *http://www.netgear.com/*

Also worth checking out is 3Com at *http://www.3com.com/* and D-Link at *http://www.dlink.com/*

Organisers

Portable computing is very much the order of the day for business people on the move. A computer that runs on batteries frees the user from the desk and enables him or her to work at times when they would otherwise be passing the time of day, possibly being bored. A train journey is a typical example.

Psion

One of the companies at the forefront of personal mobile computing is Psion and their Web site is a mine of information about their products, both hardware and software, and importantly the ability to link their computer to others. Psion plc is at *http://www.psion.com/*

Apart from the official Psion site which is run by the company, there are others run by third-party software houses as well as individuals for whom mobile computing appears to be their hobby.

Palm Pilot

The Palm series of computers is quite different from the Psion solution in so far as the machines don't have a keyboard. Instead they have just half-a-dozen buttons positioned around a touch-sensitive screen. For text entry there is an on-screen keyboard.

Like the Psion organisers, the Palm models connect to the PC or Apple Mac so that data can be moved between them. For more information about these organisers, visit *http://www.palm.com/*

Third-party applications

This site contains software upgrades that can be freely downloaded.

Both Psion and Palm have a huge following of supporters who not only use the computers, they also produce software for them. There are several sites which distribute software which is either free, or very cheap. Try PDACentral at *http://pdacentral.com/* for software and further information about Personal Digital Assistants.

Purple Software is also worth a visit – go to *http://www.purplesoft.com/*

Emulators

You can get all of the original Spectrum software to run on your PC.

Some individuals apparently prefer looking back rather than forward. In these days where 64Mb is the norm, and 32 bit operating systems with 300MHz processors are regarded as a minimum requirement, the Spectrum site takes us back to the early 1980s when the 8bit Sinclair Spectrum with 48K of memory and 8 colours was everyone's dream. I had one, and most of my friends had one. If you were involved in computing in any form at that time, chances are you had one too.

The Spectrum site offers news, views and general enthusiasm about this great little computer as well as providing all the software ever published for it. No, you don't need a tape recorder to load it: you can save it all onto disc and install the purpose-built ZX Emulator to run it on your PC.

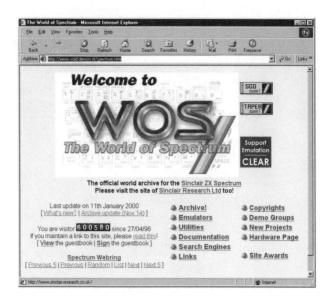

Check out this FTP directory listing: ftp:// ftp.gns. getronics.nl/ pub/os/sinclair/games.

An emulator basically fools a computer into thinking that it's something it isn't. In this case, your PC is fooled into thinking it's a 48K Spectrum (which I would have thought must be a fairly traumatic experience for the PC).

The World of Spectrum is at *http://www.void.demon.nl/ spectrum.html.*

Anti-virus software

I often wonder if the same people who write the anti-virus software are actually responsible for some of the viruses in the first place! Now there's a thought.

It's a great shame that so many intelligent people feel the need to apply their skills in such a negative way. But, viruses exist and so you need to be protected against them, especially when downloading files from the Internet.

The Virus Information site will help you sort out what you've got and what you need to get rid of it and stay rid of it.

Check this site out very carefully and make sure you're properly
protected.

Apart from the information about the various viruses, there is also free software to download. The website is at *http://www.hitchhikers.net/antivirus/*

Also look at Sophos at *http://www.sophos.com/* for further information about their virus protection software.

Computer supplies

The cost doesn't end when you buy a computer. If nothing else, you'll need paper. You may also require hardware add-ons and other consumables like floppy discs.

The rise of the home computer has also seen the rise of companies offering peripherals and consumables. Like Action (*http://www.action.com/*) many now have their own website from which online ordering is possible. Online ordering is frequently faster, but it can take longer to fill out the online order form. Also check out Misco (*http://www.misco.co.uk/*) and Viking (*http://www.vikingdirect.com/*).

These sites are also great for keeping abreast of the latest consumer items.

It's worth shopping around to get the best prices.

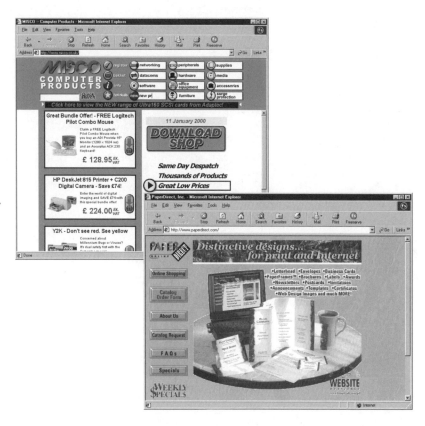

Paper Direct (*http://www.paperdirect.com/*) supply a range of pre-printed papers onto which you add the text. It's a sort of ready-made corporate image.

Computer sites

Adobe
For computer photo-retouching, as well as their world-famous Acrobat file handling software, visit Adobe at *http://www.adobe.com/*

Apple
Apple computers are very popular. Their new range of iMac computers are both stylish and easy to use. Apple are at *http://www.apple.com/*

Casio
Probably more famous for calculators and watches than computers, Casio do, however, produce some very powerful organisers. Find out more at *http://www.casio.com/*

Citizen
Citizen produce a superb range of printers and other computer peripherals. See their full range at *http://www.citizen.co.uk/*

 There's free software at many of these sites.

Compaq
http://www.compaq.com/ is the home of Compaq – probably one of the most successful computer hardware manufacturers.

Corel
CorelDRAW! – one of the most famous vector drawing programs – is by Corel. Find out more at *http://www.corel.com/*

IBM
IBM's roots go back to 1888 when Herman Hollerith suggested using a punchcard system to process results from the US census of that year. IBM are at *http://www.ibm.com/*

Intel
The processor (or CPU, as it is usually referred to) is rather like the engine of a car – the more powerful it is, the faster it goes. At the forefront of processor design is Intel. Their website is at *http://www.intel.com/*

Iomega

Specialising in high-capacity removable storage, Iomega are at *http://www.iomega.com/*

Microsoft

The most famous, largest, wealthiest and probably most 'knocked' company on the face of the Earth is Microsoft. Their website is at *http://www.microsoft.com/*

Symantec

Symantec produce a variety of anti-virus aids and tools to make Windows work better. Visit them at *http://www.symantec.com/*

Tiny Computers

Tiny Computers produce, package and market complete home PC solutions including a printer, scanner and, in some cases, a Web camera. Tiny's website is *http://www.tiny.com/*

Xara

Most of this software can be purchased over the Net.

Xara is a small software producer who has written some superb graphics programs as well as software for Web publishing. To find out more, visit Xara at *http://www.xara.com/*

ZDNet

ZDNet at *http://www.hotfiles.zdnet.com/* is the site to visit for anything to do with computers and technology in general. The highlights are reviews of the latest gadgets and gizmos, and up-to-the-minute news from the world of computing.

Computer help

With computer software becoming evermore sophisticated, and manuals becoming evermore sketchy, computer assistance has become big business. There are countless sites offering online help, advice and support on a wide range of software and hardware.

It's sometimes quicker to sort out the problem yourself.

You will find the solution to many of your computer problems in the appropriate title from the 'in easy steps' series.

See the inside-back cover for details.

Ask the Experts	—	*http://www.zdnet.com/zdhelp*
Experts Exchange	—	*http://www.experts-exchange.com/*
Help Site	—	*http://help-site.com/*
No Wonder	—	*http://www.nowonder.com/*
PC Help Online	—	*http://www.pchelponline.com/*
Support Help	—	*http://www.supporthelp.com/*

Mobile communications

Just as the service providers have established themselves in the relatively new Internet market, so too have the manufacturers of the actual phones.

As with all microelectronics, advances in technology have enabled the phones to become so small they can now fit into a shirt pocket or a handbag with ease.

Manufacturing companies like Nokia continue to take full advantage of all technological innovations, but also take the time to style the phone so that it is no longer a purely functional rectangle, but also a form which is actually pleasant to look at and comfortable to use.

The Nokia site now includes the game featured on many of their phones.

These sites are run by mobile phone manufacturers.

Ericsson phones — *http://www.ericsson.com/*

Motorola phones — *http://www.mot.com/*

Nokia phones — *http://www.nokia.com/*

Bicycles

The common pushbike has hardly changed from the day it was invented. The layout is much the same as it has always been, and only recently have new technologies brought about changes to the frame design.

Modern bikes are very comfortable and a great way to exercise.

Whether cycling on the road or over a mountain, always wear the correct gear.

Raleigh are one of the oldest bicycle manufacturers and their website at *http://www.raleigh.co.uk/* details their models and many of their manufacturing techniques.

Newer companies like Diamondback have developed bikes for fun rather than just a cheap means of transport. Their ATBs (All-Terrain Bikes) use light, but immensely strong alloy for the frame and wheels. Visit them at *http://www. diamondback.com/*

The most famous bicycle event is the Tour de France and information is available at *http://www.letour.fr/*

Watches

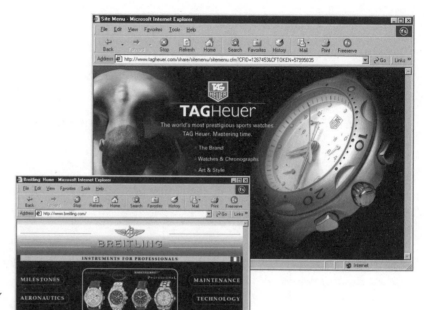

These are primarily commercial sites although they frequently contain some interesting facts.

Digital watches are very clever, but a really good-quality timepiece is something very special indeed. Modern battery powered mechanical watches are works of art. They are also extremely accurate. Check out the sites below, one of which contains some surprises.

Breitling	—	*http://www.breitling.com/*
Citizen	—	*http://www.citizenwatch.com/*
Seiko	—	*http://www.seiko.com/*
Sekonda	—	*http://www.sekonda.com/*
TAG Heuer	—	*http://www.tagheuer.com/*
Timex	—	*http://www.timex.com/*

Hi-Fi

Consumer electronics have come a long way since Akia Morita exported tape recorders under the name Sony. More than any other Japanese manufacturer, Sony dispelled the image of Japanese goods being cheap imitations of European products.

The websites of these companies primarily exist to advertise their products, but they are slick works of art that are a pleasure to navigate.

Although these sites are frequently little more than catalogues, they are always up to date.

Akai	—	*http://www.akai.com/*
Alpine	—	*http://www.alpine-europe.com/*
Hitachi	—	*http://www.hitachi.com/*
JVC	—	*http://www.jvc-europe.com/*
Sharp	—	*http://www.sharp.co.jp/index-e.html*
Sony	—	*http://www.sony.com/*
Technics	—	*http://www.technics.com/*

Cameras

To view this site, point to: http://www. polaroid.com.

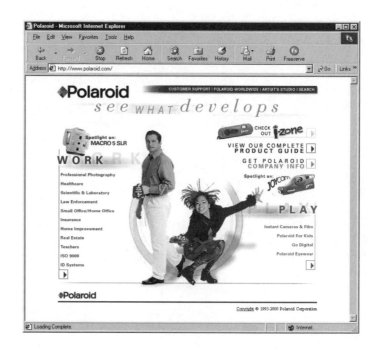

Polaroid's site not only contains information about their range of cameras, but also about the technology behind the cameras invented by Dr. Edwin Land that develop the film themselves and spit out finished photographs.

This technology was leading edge when a marketable Land camera was launched in the 1960s. In the late 1990s digital cameras were rapidly gaining ground.

A digital camera records the image not on film, but onto a small floppy disc, or more recently directly into memory. The image can then be displayed on a television or a computer, can be printed and can even be stored on a recordable CD-ROM.

For the more adventurous, the pictures can be loaded into a photo-retouching program for some fancy effects to be added.

Only time will tell whether digital cameras will totally replace conventional cameras which use rolls of film and expensive processing.

Photographic websites

Agfa	—	*http://www.agfa.com/*
Canon UK	—	*http://www.canon.co.uk/*
Casio	—	*http://www.casio.co.uk/*
Fuji Film	—	*http://www.fujifilm.com/*
Kodak	—	*http://www.kodak.co.uk/*
Minolta	—	*http://www.minolta.co.uk/*
Nikon	—	*http://www.nikon.com/*
Olympus	—	*http://www.olympus-europa.com/*
Olympus Digital	—	*http://www.olympusdigital.co.uk/*
Pentax	—	*http://www.pentax.co.uk/*
Polaroid	—	*http://www.polaroid.com/*
Ricoh	—	*http://www.ricoh-cameras.co.uk/*

Not only are there many sites from the manufacturers of cameras, there are also sites about photography.

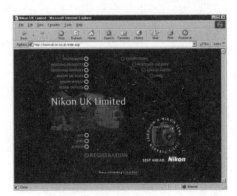

Holography	—	*http://www.holograms.co.uk/*
Time Lapse Photography	—	*http://www.gn.apc.org/maxim*
Ultimate Camera Page	—	*http://szym.com/cameras*

Travel and tourism

We pack as many of our belongings as we can into a case that we can only just carry, and then get someone to take us to the railway station. Once there we wait for hours because the train has been cancelled. Eventually we get to the airport for another interminable wait before being marched onto an aeroplane to be whisked to another part of the world. Meanwhile, scores of equally mad foreign individuals have done exactly the same to get to the place we've just left!

Covers

Chapter Twenty-Two

Getting there

Cheap Flights

Holidays can be an expensive business, especially if you've got a couple of children to take. One way of cutting the cost of international travel is to go to a company that specialises in discount tickets. Cheap Flights is one such company. Their website lists thousands of seats on hundreds of flights.

Cheap Flights can be found at *http://www.cheapflights.com/*

Plan well ahead to avoid delays and disappointments.

Star Alliance

More up-market is Star Alliance who can book you onto most of the world's major airlines and consequently to most destinations. Visit *http://www.star-alliance.com/*

Ryan Air

Ryan Air is a budget airline flying out of Stanstead and Luton to many European cities. No frills, no gimmicks, they just get you there cheaply and efficiently. Visit *http:// www.ryanair.com/* and book online.

Modern coaches are equipped with video to keep the kids and the parents amused.

Coach Travel

Travelling overland by coach is much slower than aeroplane, or even car. But you do get to see the countryside.

Wallace Arnold have been coaching people all over Europe and beyond for years. To find out what they have to offer, including rates and times, take a trip to *http://www.wallacearnold.com/*

Train travel is generally faster than coach, and you still get to see the scenery.

Train travel

Let the train take the strain, is the familiar expression. To find out what train services are available, the costs and even online booking for all the UK's railways, visit *http://www.thetrainline.com/*

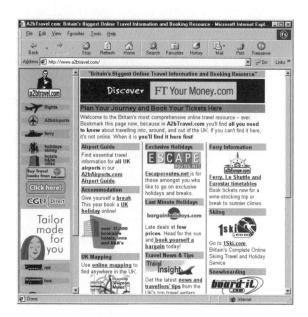

The information in these sites is updated very regularly which means it should be very accurate.

A2b Travel

This is a service which allows customers to find the times of trains, planes and ferries and then to book them.

But it's not just travel: you can also book complete holidays on the Internet as well as accommodation. You can even get the local weather report. To find a2b Travel enter *http://www.a2btravel.com/*

Places to stay

Eurocamp

Personally I've never liked sleeping under canvas, especially when I wake up freezing cold in the middle of the night and remember I've got a perfectly good bed 500 miles away. But with Eurocamp you can, if you wish, detach yourself from nature and not stay under canvas. They have a great many camp sites throughout Europe which provide mobile homes and chalets.

Camping isn't necessarily sleeping on cold damp grass.

The term 'mobile' is something of a misnomer because there isn't anything mobile about them other than the fact that they can be moved around the site with a great deal of effort and a rather large crane. These are extremely comfortable homes that just happen to be on wheels and should not be confused with a caravan that can be towed by the family car.

The chalets, too, are very spacious and feature all the mod-cons one probably has at home.

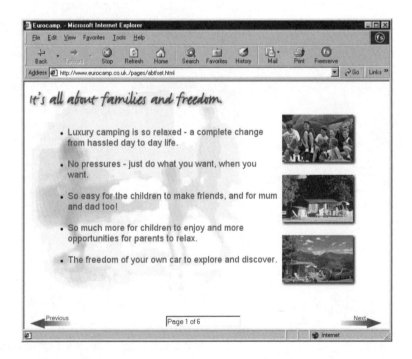

The Eurocamp website is at *http://www.eurocamp.co.uk/*

Bowhills

An alternative to a campsite is a villa or a gîte: a house for one or more families in a picturesque part of France either by the sea or inland.

These are great for two families to take a joint holiday.

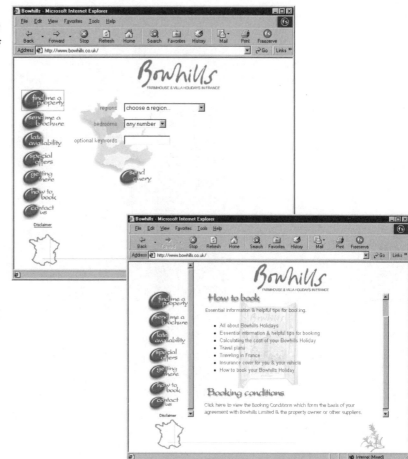

If two families are holidaying together, they need to get on really well.

Bowhills specialises in renting villas and gîtes and their website lists many. After opening the site, the first major page contains a map of France with a description about each area. Click on the area of France you're interested in and you get a list of villas with a description and price for each.

The Bowhills website is at *http://www.bowhills.co.uk/*

Hotels

If you feel you're past the age where lying on damp grass is seen as an adventure and you want something a little more up-market, then clearly you're looking for a hotel. Booking hotels in advance can be difficult and time consuming if you don't know what is available in the place you're heading to.

If you're planning a business trip, take a look at this site first.

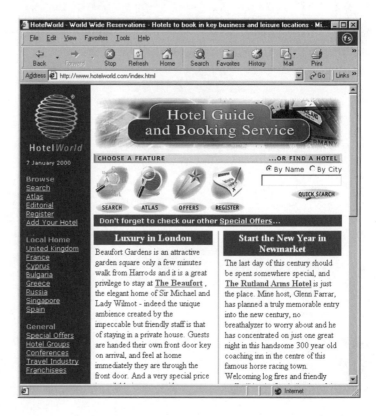

Hotel World lists all the major hotels throughout the world. A hotel can be searched for by either name or location and can then be booked online. Many of the hotels have quite a lengthy editorial about them and the website features special discounts and offers on specific hotels at particular times.

Hotel World can be found at *http://www.hotelworld.com/* All Hotels offer similar services and are at *http://www.all-hotels.com/*

Bed and Breakfast

B&B allows you to plan your day to suit yourself, not the set meal-times of the guest house.

There is something peculiarly British about Bed & Breakfast. Other countries have the equivalent, but when one thinks of B&B it immediately conjures up pictures of seaside towns and little old ladies locking the front door at 10:30 and serving bacon and eggs for breakfast.

To find out more about what B&B is really like, visit *http://www.beduk.co.uk/* or *http://www.visitus.co.uk/*

Planning and booking

Concierge

Some people love shopping around for their holiday, buying a bit here and bit there. If you have neither the time nor inclination to operate this way and want to get the whole holiday from one place, take a trip to the Concierge website.

Look through this site carefully before making any plans.

You can choose your location, make your travel plans and even chat to other would-be holiday makers in the Forum section.

Whether it's a family holiday or a romantic weekend for two, Concierge is likely to have something to suit at *http://www.concierge.com/*

Cruises

If all this seems too tourist-oriented, and the prospect of fighting for a plot on an overcrowded and overheated beach is too much, then how about a cruise?

P&O have a website at which you can find out about their cruises, from short breaks to lengthy world cruises. P&O Cruises are at *http://www.pocruises.com/*

Ensure you have currency for every country you expect to visit.

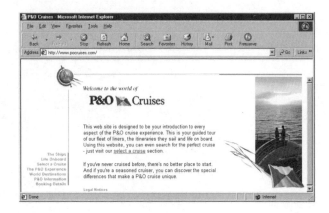

Currency

If you go to foreign parts you'll need foreign money and one of the best names for currency is Thomas Cook. Their site features a handy currency converter and lots of helpful tips. They are at *http://www.thomascook.com/*

Get your foreign currency in plenty of time, especially if it's for a non-EC country.

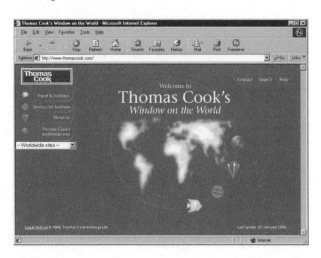

Preparation

My late uncle had the notion that if you want to make yourself understood in foreign parts, you just have to speak slowly and loudly.

HOT TIP

Don't assume everyone speaks English. Make an effort to speak their language.

If you're thinking of travelling to France for a holiday, first take the time to visit Bonjour! This site contains a huge amount of information about France and French customs, including places to stay and language help.

Similar sites exist for most countries...

Spain — *http://www.spanishabroad.com/spain.htm*

Italy — *http://www.mi.cnr.it/WOI/woiindex.html*

France — *http://www.europe-france.com/*

Holland — *http://www.visitholland.com/*

...cont'd

TravLang

If you're going to travel abroad, you should make some effort to communicate in the native language and not just assume everyone will speak English – even though they probably do.

You don't have to take a full course. There are sections for tourists.

TravLang offer would-be visitors to foreign parts a great deal of help with language. You don't have to embark on a complete course, there is a really handy section especially for travellers. TravLang may be found at *http://www. travlang.com/languages.*

The Passport

http://www.thepassport.co.uk/ is the Internet travel site for women where you can collect objective up-to-date information and advice on everything from days out to package holidays. Online booking is available, as well as a family hotel guide, and holiday horrors.

Other travel sites

World of Travel

Visit *http://www.worldoftravel.net/* for information about every form of travel from flight times to car rental, from coach tours to accommodation.

Streetfinder

This is a superb site – type in a postcode or OS grid reference and up comes a full colour map of the area. Visit *http://www.streetmap.co.uk/* for UK address or *http://www.streetmap.com/* for US addresses.

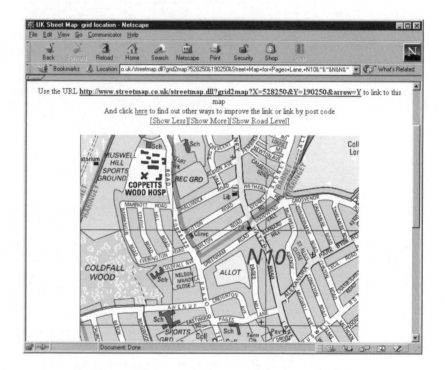

Last minute booking

Some people like to leave their bookings to the very last minute in the hope of picking up something cheap. If this is your style, a visit to *http://www.lastminute.com/* will prove beneficial.

Holiday Deals

Not just full holidays, but short stay deals at low prices. For a bargain break, visit *http://www.holidaydeals.com/*

Bargain Holidays

Open seven days a week, Bargain Holidays lets you choose your ideal getaway at sensible prices. Visit *http://www.bargainholidays.com/* to find your bargain holiday.

Sun Seeker Holidays

If you like lounging around on a sun-drenched beach, visit *http://www.sunseekerholidays.com/* to arrange your trip. Don't forget the sun-cream.

Holiday Auctions

As the name implies, you can bid for a holiday in an online auction. If you like the sound of this, visit *http://www.holidayauctions.net/* to find out how to do it.

1Ski

If you like to get away for the winter break, *http://www.1ski.com/* is a complete one-stop-shop for all your skiing and snowboarding needs. There are even links to webcams on the pistes so you can see what you're letting yourself in for.

Enforced travel

Whilst for many, travel to exotic lands is a voluntary activity, it appears that a select few are forced to make a long-distance excursion.

Apparently, there is a growing number of people who have been the victims of alien abductions.

Sometimes referred to as 'the Greys', parties of aliens visit Earth and select one or two individuals for an excursion home. Once there, many have reported being subjected to medical tests. This is not unreasonable as many countries here on Earth require medicals and a series of inoculations before visitors may enter.

Don't venture out if you hear strange noises or lights in the sky.

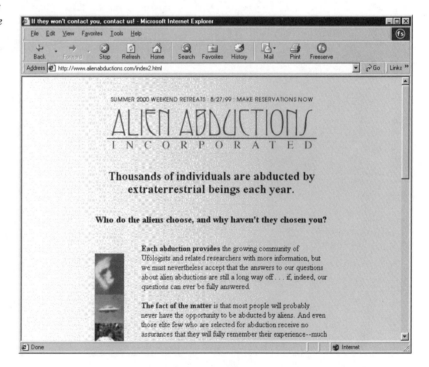

Unlike visits to other countries on Earth, most of the inter-galactic journeys have been documented. Now, these reports have been bought together in a website called Alien Abductions. If you wish to view the accounts of others or contribute an account of your own journey, visit *http:// www.alienabductions.com/*

Leisure

All work and no play makes Jack a dull boy. Too much time in front of a computer has a similar effect. Life is too short for a nonstop round of 'work, sleep, work, sleep' with nothing pleasurable in between. If you have a leisure pursuit, the chances are you'll be able to find out more about it on the Web.

Covers

Chapter Twenty-Three

Arts

The Tate Gallery

The Tate Gallery is one of the most famous galleries in the world. If you are unable to visit the Tate in person (definitely the best idea) then you can always surf there. The site offers a great deal of information about the works on display and has an easy to find index of each artist.

There are numerous virtual museums on the Net from around the world. Find out where by going to *http://nic. icom.org/vlmp/*

Many museums and art galleries have a website. Try to visit it before visiting the museum.

Visit the Tate Gallery at *http://www.tate.org.uk/*

The Turner Prize

A cow in formaldehyde and a picture made from elephant droppings are just two of the award winners of the prestigious Turner Prize. Frankly I'm sometimes at a loss to see where the art comes in, but I'm just a simple writer.

See who's won what at *http://www.tate.org.uk./info/ menui_p2.htm.*

Hi-tech art

In complete contrast to the masterpieces created with oil and canvas, there is the fantastic Embryosys website.

If you've got a really good printer, and the desire, these can be printed and framed.

Embryosys is a gallery of computer-generated pictures that look as though they were inspired by someone's really bad nightmare. There are also some amazing animations to be viewed.

Visit Embryosys at *http://embryosys.qgl.org/*

Cultural locator

If, after visiting Embryosys, you feel in need of something a little less frantic, try visiting a virtual gallery.

Although second best to visiting the real place, it is sometimes useful to have a virtual visit before having an actual visit.

Try looking at *http://www.culturefinder.com/* to find the location of such classic art galleries as The Louvre and The Hermitage.

Foundation for the Arts European is also well worth visiting at *http://www.artineurope.com/*

Theatre, ballet and opera

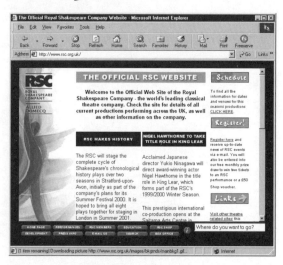

The world famous Royal Shakespeare Company has its own website listing current productions. If you register, regular updates will be sent to you by email. Point to *http:// www.rsc.org.uk/*

Learn all about English National Ballet's plans, including forthcoming tours and all the latest press releases. Also included is the complete company list with biographies of the principals. The English National Ballet is at *http:// www.ballet.org.uk/*

Operabase is a database of 500 opera houses and festivals. You can search the Operabase for a particular singer or role, conductor or producer, and follow links to production details and reviews. Operabase is at *http://www.operabase.com/*

This is only a small sample of related websites.

The most famous opera house in the world must be the one at Sydney. Visit *http://www.soh.nsw.gov.au/* for highlights of forthcoming events, or for a superb picture of SOH in front of the shimmering waters of Sydney Harbour, visit *http:// www.oznet.net/opera/*

Playbill and Stagebill Online give the latest news on the big productions on both sides of the Atlantic. Visit *http:// www.playbill.com/* and *http://www.stagebill.com/*

Films

Newline

This site offers a great deal of background information about films and cinema, including the facility to purchase film memorabilia online.

 This is currently one of the top film-related Internet sites.

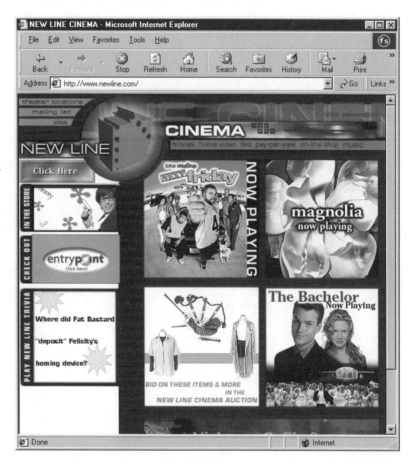

Also included in this site is information about home cinema including Digital Versatile Disc. DVD, as it is usually known, is a disc which looks similar to a conventional CD-ROM but is able to hold a great deal more data – enough for a whole feature-length film.

This is an American site so the information tends to be for that audience, but it's nevertheless worth a visit. Newline is at *http://www.newline.com/*

The Internet Movie Database

This site was started over 10 years ago, but in 1998 became a part of the Amazon family of companies. It contains information about a huge number of films. The catalogue contains all sorts of information on over 200,000 movie & TV titles as well as entertaining snippets about over 400,000 actors and actresses and 40,000 directors.

There is a powerful search facility to help you find exactly what you're looking for, be it an actor, film title or even a plot.

This is a rapidly expanding site.

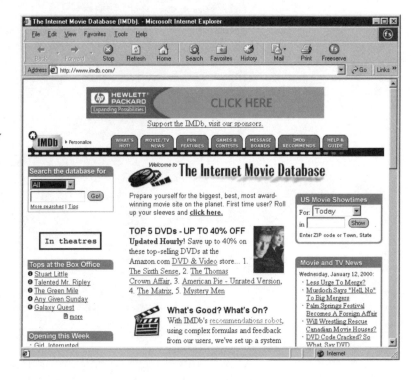

The Internet Movie Database may be found by entering *http://www.imdb.com/*

For fans of cult movies (i.e. the ones with no story line) the Cult Movies Checklist is at *http://cs.bilkent.edu.tr/~tugrul/cult.html*

Other movie sites

Although shamelessly plugging their own products, the Sony Pictures Entertainment site offers a great deal to the movie buff. Information about home cinema, television and a superb studio tour make this one of the top movie sites. SPE is at *http://www.spe.sony.com/movies*.

A good review doesn't always mean it is going to be an enjoyable film.

Ain't It Cool Movie Reviews at *http://www.aint-it-cool-news.com/* contains reviews of some of the classic movies.

The Warner Brothers website is the place to go for everything about the latest films. They even have a really cute mouse pointer. Warner Brothers are at *http://www.movies.warnerbros.com/*

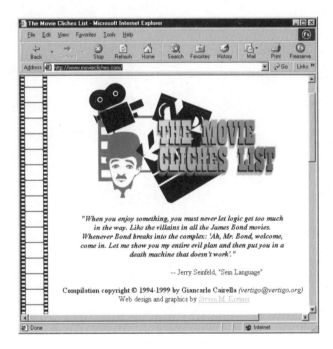

Most movie sequels contain those cringe-making lines that have the audience squirming in their seats. How many times have we heard the phrase, 'The name's Bond. James Bond.' For more of this, visit Movie Cliches at *http://www.moviecliches.com/*

Science fiction

Before starting on a search of the Internet for Science Fiction sites, take a look at the Science Fiction Foundation Collection at *http://www.liv.ac.uk/~asawyer/sf_info.html*. It lists most sites on the subject.

Star Trek

Since Captain Kirk and his crew set out on a 5 year mission to go where no man had gone before, a whole industry has grown up around Star Trek. There are countless Star Trek sites but the official one is at *http://www.startrek.com/*

Visit these sites to get all the background facts and little known trivia.

Star Wars

So it transpires that the original Star Wars was actually Episode 4. The next two sequels were Episodes 5 and 6. The makers, seemingly running out of ideas for more sequels, began making prequels and Episode 1 was launched some 20 years after the original Star Wars (which became Episode 4). I'm sure money had nothing to do with it.

Like Star Trek, there are countless sites dedicated to Star Wars, but there is only one official site and that is at *http://www.starwars.com/*

The X-Files

The Official X-Files website is typical of these official Sci-Fi websites. It contains a huge amount of background material on the series including interesting snippets about the stars.

Producers of hit shows like The X-Files waste no time in opening a website to deal with the interest the show inevitably generates. In this site there's a full guide to each of the episodes as well as background information about the storylines.

Don't read this just before going to bed!

For those who are really keen, there's the chance to buy some useful items connected with the show. The official X-Files are at *http://www.thex-files.com/*

If you're really interested in buying memorabilia or collectables from a Sci-Fi film or TV series, then the Sci-Fi UK Superstore should be your first port of call at *http:// www.scifi-uk.com/*

Television

Television is going through something of a revolution. Having enjoyed what is now referred to as Terrestrial TV for over 40 years, this is no longer good enough. Satellite dishes became the pollution of the 80's and Cable TV followed soon after. Now the buzz-words of the moment are *wide-screen*, *video-on-demand* and *digital*.

All of the major TV companies have a website in which they give programme times and additional or background information about their programmes.

Most TV companies have their own website.

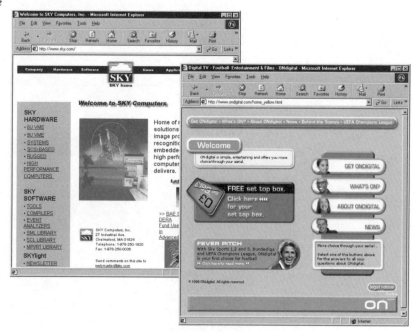

This is only a small sample of related websites.

BBC TV	—	*http://www.bbc.co.uk/*
Channel 4	—	*http://www.channel4.co.uk/*
Carlton	—	*http://www.carlton.co.uk/*
Central	—	*http://www.centraltv.co.uk/*
Sky	—	*http://www.sky.co.uk/channel/intro.htm*
On Digital	—	*http://www.ondigital.com/*

Television programmes

Soaps

Many television programmes have their own website. In most cases there is a link from the site of the television company which screens the programme.

Not all TV websites are the official ones – some are run by fans.

Soaps are popular on TV and also on the Web as they frequently give 'the story so far'. Typical is Neighbours at *http://www.neighbours.com/* (this also gives information about the characters).

Satellite TV has enabled these programmes to be fed into homes around the world.

Other popular soap sites are...

Coronation Street	—	*http://www.coronationstreet.co.uk/*
Eastenders	—	*http://www.bbc.co.uk/eastenders/*
Brookside	—	*http://www.brookie.com/*
Soap Heaven	—	*http://www.geocities.com/ TelevisionCity/2533*

At the Brookside site, you can also opt to receive updates by email.

Television for grown-up children

There are numerous programmes that started out as being for children but later gained a cult following among adults.

One of the first TV programmes I remember watching as a child was a series of 10 minute stories about a little boy with a magic light on his head. His name was Torchie the Battery Boy. This was Gerry Anderson's first puppet programme and was followed in the early 1960's with Four Feather Falls – an altogether slicker production insofar as it was harder to see the strings.

Information about all of Anderson's programmes, (including the live-action ones) is here.

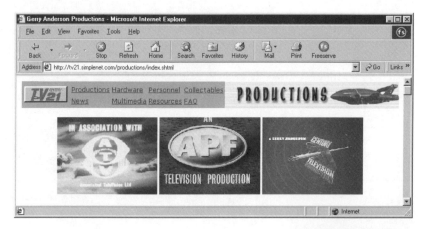

His programmes really started to gather a following with Supercar and then Fireball XL5. (And if you can remember the words to the closing captions, you're older than you're letting on!)

This site contains links to other sites selling models and memorabilia.

The really big break came with Thunderbirds – the story of 5 sons, a widowed father in a wheelchair and fantastic tales of daring rescues.

Visit Gerry Anderson's home page at *http://tv21.simplenet.com/* and remind yourself of the programmes, the characters and the machinery.

Cartoons

Love it or hate it, the Simpsons is currently one of the most popular TV cartoons and its website is also one of the most popular.

Sites like this can add a great deal of enjoyment to the programme by providing a considerable amount of additional information about characters and the way it is made.

In the UK, Nick Park's Wallace & Gromit series of stop-motion animations also have a loyal army of fans all apparently armed with their own website.

If you've never watched The Simpsons, don't bother visiting this site.

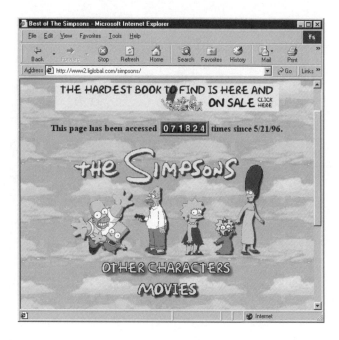

The Simpsons	—	*http://www2.liglobal.com/simpsons*
Captain Pugwash	—	*http://rummelplatz.uni-mannheim. de/~mfeld/wg_home.html*
Captain Pugwash	—	*http://www2.prestel.co.uk/orton/ pugwash/*
South Park	—	*http://www.comedycentral.com/southpark*

Classic TV programmes

There is a great deal of interest in TV programmes from the 60's, 70's and 80's. Many of them from these decades are enjoying reruns and even re-reruns. Some stand up to time very well, others look decidedly dated.

The Sweeney is still very watchable and is enjoyed by many, although I do find it slightly embarrassing – I used to dress that way too! The Sweeney is at *http://www.thesweeney.com/*

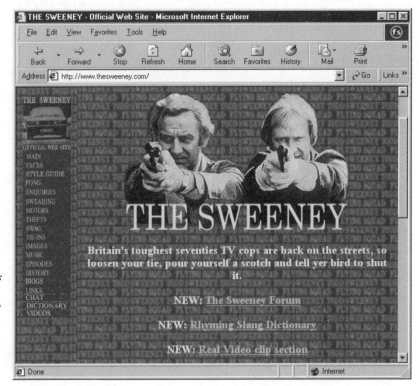

Satellite TV has enabled these programmes to be fed into homes around the world.

The Avengers	—	*http://www.originalavengers.com/home.html*
British TV	—	*http://www.uktv.com/*
Classic 70's & 80's UK kids' TV	—	*http://www.geocities.com/TelevisionCity/1011/index.html*

Fan pages

There are many people around the world whose passion for a particular TV series knows no bounds. Wearing little more than an anorak, armies of fans spend untold hours building a sort of electronic shrine to their passion, which is apparently collecting little-known trivia about obscure TV programmes.

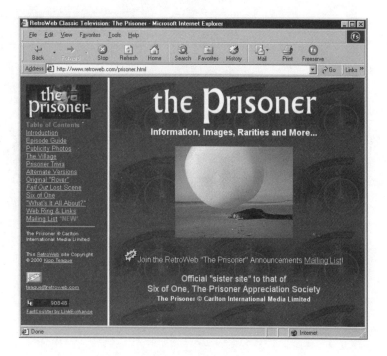

The more weird or offbeat the subject, the more websites it attracts.

The Prisoner had a completely incomprehensible storyline set in the mock Italian village of Portmeirion, Wales. The website is *http://www.retroweb.com/prisoner.html.*

The incomprehensible feature of 1960's soap Crossroads was why anyone should ever have wanted to watch it. But if you still crave after Benny, Miss Diane, Amy and Meg, visit *http://www.geocities.com/TelevisionCity/2603.*

The Saint, by Leslie Charteris, featured the overactive eyebrow of Roger Moore in the title role. To catch up on all the trivia, visit *http://www.saint.org/*

Sport

Whatever your preference, whether a spectator or an active participant, your sport will be on the Web somewhere.

Visit this site for the latest information about the next Olympic Games.

While some sites are almost permanent fixtures, others are published for a specific sporting event and are then removed, or at the very least forgotten forever.

Currently the sports site that is receiving a great deal of attention is the Olympics 2000 site at *http://www. olympics.com/eng/* although once the 2000 Olympics are over the site will doubtless change in readiness for the next Games, 4 years hence.

Until fairly recently this website was a little sparse in places but, as the time of the Olympics draws nearer, it has increased in size quite dramatically.

Here you will be able to find all the latest news leading up to the big event. The site is regularly updated and is probably the leading source of information about the next Olympic Games.

Motor sport

If, like me, you enjoy spending Sunday afternoons watching indistinguishable cars being hammered by faceless drivers round and round featureless Tarmac circuits, then the Web has plenty of sites to look at.

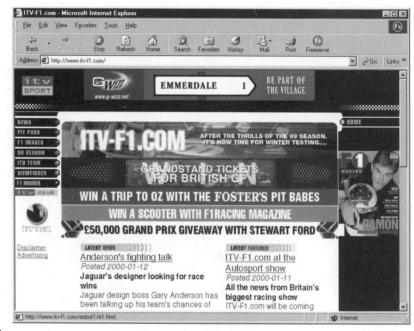

These sites are updated very frequently.

These are some other top motor sport sites to visit.

Formula 1 coverage has improved considerably in recent years. In the UK, ITV has the screening rights at present. To back up their coverage, they have a website at *http://www.itv-f1.com/*

NASCAR features American saloon car racing, usually on oval tracks and at very high speed. To keep up to date with the latest stories, visit *http://www.nascar.com/*

The majority of Formula 1 teams have their own websites e.g.:

• *Jordan – http://www. jordangp.com/*

• *Ferrari – http://www. shell-ferrari.com/*

• *McLaren – http://www. mclaren.com/*

FIA, the international governing body for motor sport, have a dual language (French and English) website at *http://www.fia.com/*

Football

Not all clubs in the football division have their own website, but of those that do Arsenal's must be regarded as one of the very best. Built onto a background of a piece of electronic gadgetry, presumably something to do with their sponsor, the design and layout of the site are a model of perfection.

This is how a website should be constructed and maintained. Supporters of other clubs must be very envious.

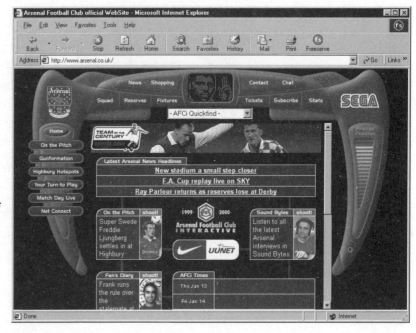

Check out this site regularly as it is frequently updated.

The site holds information about the club, their games, their victories and the players – in fact, just about everything about the club.

It is regularly updated with in-depth stories about recent matches as well as previews of forthcoming matches.

Arsenal's website is at *http://www.arsenal.co.uk/* whilst FIFA's is *http://www.fifa.com/*

The other top website is that of Manchester United at *http://www.manutd.co.uk/*

Other sporting sites

The list goes on and on, but these are some of the top sports sites.

Badminton	—	*http://www2.mozcom.com/ ~arielf/sport/links.html*
CricInfo	—	*http://www-uk.cricket.org/*
IGolf	—	*http://www.igolf.com/*
Tennis	—	*http://www.tennis.com/*
Snooker	—	*http://www.snookernet.com/ wwwsnooker/*
Runners World	—	*http://www.runnersworld.com/*
Wimbledon	—	*http://www.wimbledon.org/*
SailNet	—	*http://sailing.org/*
Scuba.Net	—	*http://www.scubaworld.com/*
Swimnews	—	*http://www.swimnews.com/*
UK Diving	—	*http://www.ukdiving.co.uk/*
SkiNet	—	*http://www.skinet.com/*
Skiing Listing	—	*http://skicentral.com/*
British Horse Soc.	—	*http://www.equiworld.net/*
International Rugby Football	—	*http://www.irfb.com/*

This is only a small sample of websites for sporting activities.

Music

If music be the food of love, play on. The subjects of the music pages range from artists and composers to record companies and song listings.

The Beatles

At the last count, there were about 500 Beatles websites – and that's not counting the foreign language ones. Selecting just one was really difficult but of them all, *http://members.aol.com/LuvBeatlez/beatles.htm* looks about the best with pages about each member, albums, films and, of course, the songs.

Use the search engines to find information about your favourite groups and artists.

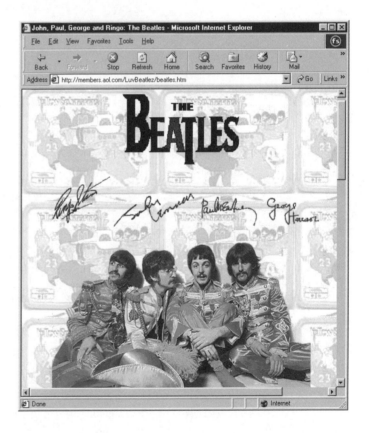

The Rolling Stones

Billed as the greatest Rock and Roll band in the world, The Rolling Stones are also the longest running Rock and Roll band in the world. Find out more at *http://www.therolling-stones.com/*

Queen

This amazing supergroup produced some of the greatest rock anthems of the 1970's and 1980's. Everything you want to know about the band, the songs and the shows is at *http://queen.frnet.com/*

Group search

Most groups and solo artists of the 1950's, 1960's, 1970's and 1980's can be located by going to a special site. Once there you'll be presented with the letters of the alphabet. Click on the initial letter of the artist's name and you'll get a list of artists beginning with that letter, from which you should find the one you're looking for. Point to *http://music.netscape.com/*

Classical sites

The Internet caters for all tastes – from Heavy Rock to Heavy Classical. There are countless websites devoted to classical music but, for me, the pick is Impulse Music at *http://www.impulse-music.co.uk/*

Founded, designed and maintained by two musicians whose love of music just oozes out of the site, Impulse is increasing in popularity with hits from all around the world.

Tutti

Tutti is the musical term used to indicate that everybody is to play, and this site aims to do exactly that – enable every musician with a CD, sheet music, book or other musically related item to distribute it to a global market.

Tutti (*http://www.tutti.co.uk/*) is a Web shop-window for classical music. Composers, musicians, record labels and publishers offer their goods for sale by credit card transaction on a digitally secure site provided by Impulse.

Other musical sites

Classical Choice	—	*http://www.cdchoice.com/*
Classical Insites	—	*http://www.classicalinsites.com/*
Classical MIDI Archives	—	*http://www.prs.net/midi.html*
Maestronet Home Page	—	*http://www.maestronet.com/*
The British Music Page	—	*http://syweb.easynet.co.uk/ ~snc/british.htm*
Virgin	—	*http://channels.virgin.net/ channels/intro.html*
Vitaminic	—	*http://www.vitaminic.com/*

Index